DESIGN/BUILD
WITH JERSEY DEVIL

DESIGN/BUILD
WITH JERSEY DEVIL

A Handbook for Education and Practice

Charlie Hailey

Princeton Architectural Press
New York

Contents

SPEAK OF THE DEVIL

HANDBOOK

Speak of the devil, and there it is. Talking can summon the object of discussion, and nowhere is this truer than in the studio and on the construction site. When designing, we talk about the methods a builder might use to construct a tricky corner joint. We imagine how it will come together by feeling the weight of the wood and reading its grain, and then we draw the notch as if we were the ones cutting it. When building, we lay out footings as a prevailing breeze reminds us of the design's orientation, conjuring up the designer's many drafts of the site plan.

Design and construction haunt each other, and never have I been more attuned to these connections than in my conversations with the members of Jersey Devil. Jim Adamson, Steve Badanes, and John Ringel remind us that intertwining design and build is not just relevant but also essential. **Fig. 01** The moment we breathe intentions into design, we are building. And while we build, design is there at our elbow.

Fig. 01 Jersey Devil is Steve Badanes (left), Jim Adamson (middle), and John Ringel (right). This photograph was taken in a vintage prairie schooner at their camp known as the "Secret Location" near Yestermorrow Design/Build School, where they teach summer design/build courses.

This book discusses how teaching design/build operates. It calls upon the expertise of Jersey Devil to unpack the devilish premise that design and construction are not distinct. As a primer and a handbook for teaching, it lays out pedagogical tools, processes, and outcomes with reference to Jersey Devil's work. As an Architecture Brief, this book combines the didactic immediacy of an architect's and a builder's pocket companion with the insights and problem-solving voices of the studio.

Handbooks should be handy. My hope is that readers, as makers, will take this book and use it as a kind of tool on site and in their studios and shops. To be handy does not just mean that you use your hands, although that is the starting point; it also means that you are clever in your use of those hands. Being handy combines manual and creative work, and this hyphenation in "han-di-work" binds skill with innovative action: you are able *and* you are ready to do something. Likewise, this book is ready and near at hand, matching utility with insights highlighted by Jersey Devil's experiences. Its organization and topics provide a toolkit for practicing and teaching design/build, while stories, didactic commentary, and sample exercises complement the nuts-and-bolts content.

In this first chapter, Jersey Devil's origins and ethos serve as a lens to introduce the design/build experience. The next chapter, "Groundwork," is a comprehensive look at the objectives, curriculum, and logistics of design/build: What is the ideal scope for a project? Where can we find funding? What goes into a project's preplanning? "Toolbox" then unpacks the tools, tactics, and circumstances of design/build studios. Its range includes physical and conceptual tools as well as their application. "Process" moves step-by-step through the design/build adventure, from meetings in studio to breaking ground to completing construction: What happens on day one? How do the weeks of design and construction then unfold? How do you maintain group consensus throughout?

An important thread of this handbook traces educational reform and its connection to public interest, activism, and responsibility. What does design/build pedagogy teach? How does it work? How does the process of designing and building transform its context, connect with local communities and broader society, and inform a political approach? What happens when alternate models of education—and practice—can no longer be alternatives but become essential to sustaining environments? These questions lead to the next chapter, "Lessons," which presents the outcomes of designing and building—what can be learned from its process and how design/build works in its broader social context. Three in-depth case studies, a project index, and a reading list serve as additional reference tools.

ORIGINS

There are now more than one hundred design/build programs in schools across North America, and still many more across the world. Studios that combine designing and building have, by some estimates, increased three-fold over the past two decades and now influence architecture and design curriculum more than ever before. However, in the late 1960s, much of design education remained focused solely on design. While enrolled at Princeton University—Steve and John as graduate students and Jim as an undergraduate—the collective that would eventually form Jersey Devil had to find cultures of construction outside of the institution.

Steve and John first collaborated in 1969. They designed and built play structures and inflatable constructions under the fanciful, politically charged monikers Suburban Renewal, Cloud Builders, and Midnight Construction Company. **Fig. 02** Three years later their Snail House project spawned the Jersey Devil name. **Fig. 03** The story has often been told and is now legend: shocked by seeing its spiraling plan, stacked manhole risers, curved rafters, bubble window, and (perhaps most radically) designers actually carrying out their project's construction, local residents could only believe that the devil of South Jersey folklore was at work. Jim later joined the group in 1975 to help build the Silo House. **Fig. 04** Jersey Devil then continued to design and build projects across North America (from New Hampshire to Baja), at a range of scales (from bookcases to houses and public structures) and for diverse clients (from steamfitters to surgeons). **Figs. 05–06**

Currently working in their fifth decade, the group's collaborators continue to make things, though now mostly with students. Steve teaches at the University of Washington, Jim has taught at MIT and Miami University and currently teaches at the University of Miami, and John teaches at Yestermorrow Design/Build School, where Jim and Steve also run a summer course. **Fig. 07** Project locations have included their institutions' respective headquarters in Seattle, South Florida, and Vermont, as well as international studios in Cambodia, Costa Rica, Cuba, El Salvador, Finland, Ghana, India, Mexico, and Taiwan. Their projects with students are diverse, open to the community, highly accessible to the general public, and of a manageable scale.

Interviewed by Michael Crosbie in 1984, Steve said he hoped to see more students building what they design. There were few design/build programs at the time, and many hands-on projects originated from community design centers. Yale's Building Workshop continued, focusing at the time on pavilion projects, Yestermorrow was newly established in 1980, and Auburn University's Rural Studio was still almost a decade away. The 1980s marked Jersey Devil's transition into not only practicing design/build but also teaching it, and Sambo Mockbee would later credit its members as inspiration for Rural Studio.

They saw the potential to convey what they were doing and what they were learning to the next generation of designers who might also become makers. Their practice already included pedagogy: each project was a "make tank" where everyone—artists, tradespeople, students, and clients—participated in the learning process that each jobsite provided. Steve hoped that students, as designers and builders, might not only be helping transform modes of practice but also "be having a lot more fun." According to the legend, the group's eponymous demon brought playful mischief to its New Jersey surroundings, and Jersey Devil's members now teach how actually building what you design can shake things up. After the group's years of globally influential work, their focus on design/build education has brought Jersey Devil full circle.

Fig. 02 Poster for Midnight Construction, March 1972.

Jersey Devil says:

" **Not agents of the dark prince, but rather those lucky—perhaps handsome—devils, having a devil of a good time, seeking the devil in the details, avoiding idle hands as we work like the devil, sometimes in a devil-may-care fashion, advocating for design/build.** " [John]

Fig. 03 Snail House under construction, Forked River, New Jersey, 1972.

Fig. 04 Silo House, Lambertville, New Jersey, 1975.

Fig. 05 Helmet House, Goffstown, New Hampshire, 1974.

Fig. 06 Casa Mariposa, Baja California, Mexico, view from the north, 1988–89.

Fig. 07 Yestermorrow Design/Build School with covered builder's yard, during Jim and Steve's Public Interest Design/Build studio, summer 2013.

ARCHITECTURE 101

Jersey Devil's commitment to teach and practice design/build came equally as a refinement and a reaction to their own architectural education—Princeton did lack a design/build program, but there also existed a sociopolitical context that urged a rethinking of how architecture would be made. As John recalls: "The first Earth Day came along and we all had a sense that there was something substantial there. Something that was not trying to justify form, but rather generated real form from real function...form coming from process, materials, and technique." That first semester Steve and John took Robert Geddes's Architecture 101. Jim, an undergraduate at the time, had recently completed this introductory course, a class that I would also take two decades later. Though expansive in content, Architecture 101 still hewed a relatively narrow role for the architect. But it was 1968—Princeton would admit women a year later, and on Monday, May 4, 1970, a protest assembly of four thousand students and faculty, John Ringel and Robert Geddes among them, hashed out Princeton Strike's resolutions. **Fig. 08**

Fig. 08 John (center right) talks with Robert Geddes at the Princeton Strike, Jadwin Gym, May 4, 1970.

Jersey Devil's future members' coursework overlapped, and they also shared studio space. The interior of Princeton's School of Architecture moves fluidly—sometimes to the grad students' vexation—from ground level to upper mezzanine. John and Steve worked upstairs, but their backgrounds in engineering and art meant they needed to take additional leveling coursework with the undergraduates, which put them into contact with Jim. He recalls that Steve took an interest in his thesis project for a floating water pollution exhibit. Critiqued by some faculty for its so-called nonarchitectural components, the ferro-cement boat signaled the work of a fellow traveler, environmentally prescient and radically demonstrative of what architecture can do.

After his first semester at Princeton, Steve drove to Warren, Vermont. Snow girded the Green Mountains, and most would think the weather a bit too cold to work outside with your hands. But there at Prickly Mountain, people were building, and Steve discovered a counterpoint to grad school's formal curriculum. He was following other Ivy League expats, including Dave Sellers, who, two years earlier, also traveled the Mad River Valley to find a place for building designs amid cheap real estate, permissive codes, and legacies of the "good life." Jim made a similar journey after graduation, traveling to Vermont to build a house and to escape what he felt was an overly academic curriculum, one too disconnected from the everyday built environment.

On their way to Vermont, Steve and David each left schools poised for change. In 1967 Charles Moore established Yale's Building Workshop, and at Princeton that same year Robert Geddes coauthored the polemical *Study of Education for Environmental Design*, which sought greater connection between academic disciplines and called for service to the broader community. Though hesitant to lay down fixed priorities, the report's authors posited these goals for students:

→ Work effectively within real-world constraints.

→ Comprehend continuing socioeconomic changes.

→ Envision better environments beyond present-day constraints.

The American Institute of Architects sponsored the study, and Geddes's report and course still framed these changes from within conventional architectural practice. But the education of these architects—Jim, John, and Steve—laid foundations for environmentally and socially expanded roles in the field. Steve's basic objectives for his design/build courses hint at Geddes's report, resonate with John Dewey's contention that education is life itself, and work from the idea that the architect's client is the whole of society:

→ Collaborative, consensus design experience

→ Learning-by-doing and real-world design

→ Development of communication skills

→ Redefinition of values—community service and commitment

LAB

New directions in curriculum alone could not house Jersey Devil's aspirations, nor could they solely structure the process of design/build. John and Steve found a place to start their alternative practice in Princeton's Architectural Laboratory. **Fig. 09** Leon Barth ran the lab for almost fifty years, signing on soon after Jean Labatut, the School of Architecture's director of graduate studies, sponsored the 1949 renovation of the Firestone family's polo stables on the south side of campus. The lab was a place for experimentation. Labatut added a sign welcoming the bricoleur and cautioning the uninitiated: "Experimental Area. Danger! Keep Out!" It was intimately tied to the school but geographically distinct, located a long walk down campus from the architecture building.

Fig. 09 Architecture Lab, Princeton University, c. 1950.

The lab was a parallel school where artists, scientists, innovators, and designer/builders felt at home. Labatut echoed Jersey Devil's own educational rubric when he described the lab's purpose in a 1952 edition of the *Daily Princetonian*:

"Learning architecture over a drawing board alone would be like becoming a chemist by just reading and never actually mixing the chemicals. And yet, we are the only ones to have built a place like this where we can experiment under natural as well as artificial conditions, finding the ultimate values of color, the effects of weathering and the relationship of architecture to the physical environment."

Leon modestly described himself as the lab's "technician" but he was more than that. John knew him as a "highly skilled craftsman" who built guitars, designed furniture, and made buildings. As "a mentor to generations of architecture students," he offered insights on everything from proper diet to precise dovetails, from restoring MG TDs to ripping MDF, and from popping chalk lines to living a full life. He had helped build Marcel Breuer's Lauck House and worked with Ben Shahn in Roosevelt, New Jersey, where he was mayor for eleven years, but he was never more thrilled than when his students successfully drove a nail to connect 2x4s in the lab's 24-foot glass cube classroom. Leon told us stories about the lab's ghosts—Buckminster Fuller's geodesic domes, the Olgyay brothers' Thermoheliodon, Steve and John's Plexiglas experiments, and Frank Lloyd Wright's spectral visit, his black cape flecked with the lab's sawdust. With Leon in the lab, Jersey Devil found a place to begin a life of learning to design and build. **Fig. 10**

Fig. 10 Steve with his Rockwell circular saw mural on the Architectural Lab's wall, 1970.

BUBBLE

Across from Princeton's Architectural Lab, John proposed an inflatable dormitory. It was the autumn of 1970, Ant Farm was setting up nomadic bubbles across the country, and *Progressive Architecture*'s C. Ray Smith was linking expanded consciousness to expanded spaciousness. Princeton's student population was growing, and with the university's admission of women a year earlier, administrators sought expanded housing. On November 8, John helped the university's Student Housing Cooperative stage an event to celebrate inflatables. Polyethylene bubbles rose more than thirty feet as bands played acid rock inside, and the organizers promoted bubble architecture as an alternative to traditional campus housing.

Fig. 11 Bubble Day at Princeton in 1969.

After the Bubble Dorm event **Fig. 11**, Mercer County commissioned Steve and John to design and build an inflatable cloud to shade New Jersey State Museum's plaza for its Teen Arts Festival. John recalls that they "inflated and suspended the bubble over the plaza, but harrowing winds" forced it to the ground, where they cut a hole in the bubble's yellow material and allowed participants to enter for a "mellow yellow" experience. Similar projects, like John's bubble structure for another Teen Arts Festival on Princeton's campus, followed, and for a

Fig. 12 Inflatable, Teen Arts Festival, New Jersey State Museum, Trenton, New Jersey, 1973.

Figs. 13–14 Inflatable, Teen Arts Festival.

time John and Steve called themselves Cloud Builders. **Figs. 12–15**

At this early point in their careers, inflatables allowed for low-cost experimentation and resonated with the antiestablishment DIY approach they advocated. For them, the mix of designing and building meant the fit of new technologies with new lifestyles and the relation of form to life's informal nature. John's *Bubble Dorm Working Paper*, though framed officially as a feasibility study for the university, included collaged illustrations for the inflatable dormitory near the Architectural Lab. **Fig. 16** In the spirit of Archigram's magazines and Ant Farm's *Inflatocookbook*, one page invokes "Kids!" to "start here…OK, gang, now it's time to do-it-yourself! And Rip Off Along Dotted Line…And Then:

1. Paste this page to an old shirtboard.
2. Cut out the modules.
3. Make your own Bubble Plan on drawing number a-5."

Design/build at your fingertips. A hands-on approach to a proposal that quite literally untethers the institution's buildings and by extension reframes the educational experience.

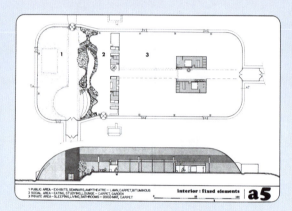

Fig. 15 Plan and Section of Bubble Dorm proposal, November 1970.

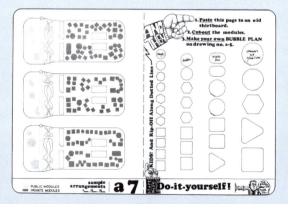

Fig. 16 Do-it-yourself Bubble Plan, *Bubble Dorm Working Paper No. 1*, John Ringel and Gus Escher, November 1970.

ROUGHING IT

When you "rough it," you live primitively—constructing a simple shelter is akin to building a good campfire. On the road and away from home, the idea of shelter comes back to basics. For John, such necessity infuses design with function and inspires how you build. If design/build has an archetype, it is surely the basic shelter: the primitive hut. Steve and Jim often lived on site in Airstreams. **Figs. 17–18** These trailers had not yet appeared in television commercials, nor did they serve as food trucks or film-set changing rooms; they were simply machines for living, ready-made domestic vessels that complemented a camp's more ad hoc constructions. In the early years, the members of Jersey Devil roughed it out of necessity, but they would have done it anyway—living on the site afforded an intimate connection to the work and a place to experiment with the project of living.

Roughing it also has applications in building. When you rough something out, you put together essential parts in order to understand how they fit and prepare for the next step. Jim's site-built structures contrasted with the Airstreams' sleekness while matching their innovation. Many were improvised from construction waste: discarded shipping boxes became the Cardboard Grotto, and extra cement slurry and mesh sculpted the Sphincter House's organic form. **Figs. 19–21** Tree houses, a modified VW van, solar showers, composting toilets, and pinwheel wind generators dotted these campsites—they were constructions within the larger construction project. **Fig. 22** I am reminded of Taliesin West students who, in the spirit of the school's original Camp Ocotillo, build their own minimal desert shelters to live in during their enrollment.

When the members of Jersey Devil teach at Yestermorrow, they camp nearby at what they call the "Secret Location," where they extend the day's lessons into evening discussions around a table in the 1954 prairie schooner, itself a memory theater of projects, wallpapered with news clippings, reference books, and sawdust-covered punch lists. The schooner's first life was as a travel trailer that has now come to rest in the mountains of central Vermont. **Figs. 23–24** On Yestermorrow's campus, some students live down the hall from the woodshop, and others pitch tents or build improvised shelters on the grounds: a community close to the work and to each other. As Steve says, "That's when you talk about design issues, right there, when it's in front of you." This familiarity, even intimacy, with a site fosters a deeper understanding of the place and extends to the social context.

Roughing it puts you close to context and, by extension, to life. Proximity to the jobsite is not merely live-plus-work—it wholly changes perspectives on labor itself: not live-work, but living work. Steve notes how embedding oneself in a locale fosters an economy of means and a frugality based on what is close at hand. And Jim finds a similar attachment to place and work site when his students live locally during projects abroad—away from home and

Fig. 17 Jim's Airstream in Baja California.

Fig. 18 Steve's Airstream in the Florida Keys.

Fig. 19 Jim's Cardboard Grotto, during construction of the Silo House.

Fig. 20 Interior of Cardboard Grotto. These projects recall Jim's earlier experiments with making things. Growing up in New Jersey, Jim built underground forts and crafted a water-ski jump that was also linked to an improvised tent city in the woods. Similarly, John recalls making cardboard models for his O-gauge Lionel train set. He also built a dog house, renovated the basement of his parents' house, and later added a carport.

Fig. 21 Sphincter House. Jim placed chicken wire over an armature of 3/8" rebar, which he then covered with burlap bags that had been dipped in a slurry of mortar. After curing, he added a layer of troweled mortar.

Fig. 22 Tree-house campsite during construction of the Football House, Woodside, California, 1976.

Fig. 23 Prairie schooner at Secret Location, Warren, Vermont.

Fig. 24 Camping platform at Secret Location.

immersed in design/build. As John points out, it is like living amidst the work of a home renovation project. Roughing it disallows distinctions of architect and contractor (you are both), drawings and constructions (you make both), and design and build (you do both).

Jersey Devil found a home with each new project. The group's mobility allowed for diverse projects in unique places, and it is not surprising that they each now anchor a corner of the country—Steve in Seattle, Jim in Miami, and John in New Jersey. Roughing it fostered Jersey Devil's itinerancy but also anchors the realities of the design/build process, of making what you conceive. True to their namesake, they made mischief while traveling from place to place, but a deep-seated ethic grounds this audacity. Outlandish forms come from alternative materials, dramatic structures soften unbuildable sites, and overt environmental systems celebrate climate responsiveness. Just as Jersey Devil roughed it on site and their constructions made possible seemingly impossible ways of living, they now bring this enthusiasm to their design/build pedagogy.

> **And what a great idea—a bunch of guys who are willing to pack up their tools, go anywhere, live on a site, and build something.** [Jim]

ETHOS: REACTIVE PRACTICE

"Jersey Devil was never about individual ideas but about a group process and collaboration. And that extended onto the jobsite. It's more inclusive—we took responsibility for our designs by building, we developed the designs together, and we built them together. I think what we accomplished is not measured so much by what we built but by how we did it." [Steve]

When Steve speaks of their work not so much in terms of what they have done as in terms of how they did it, he is indeed talking about alternative practices, but he is also outlining the core of design/build's pedagogy and the ways they continue to teach how to do it. This is not passivity; they are not waiting for things to happen before responding. It is instead an attitude that combines action with feedback: challenging preconceptions, diving into a context with tools (and skills) at hand, and learning from what you are doing—ultimately taking responsibility for what you have designed.

From the outset, Jersey Devil explored how design/build works—not only how buildings themselves function but also how the process of building informs those outcomes. This ethos infused their first decade's experiments with alternative energy and materials, along with alternative methods of delivering projects. They also pioneered architecture that responded to its environment, particularly through passive solar design. In the 1980s politics changed the context, and Steve recalls how commissions slowed as tax credits and incentives for energy conservation expired during Ronald Reagan's presidency.

A 1981 research grant from the National Endowment for the Arts afforded Steve the opportunity to study design/build, and this laid the groundwork for his first teaching gig at Ball State University. The studio context was a natural extension of Steve's fundamental interest in learning by doing, and he readily accepted John Connell's invitation for the following summer to teach the Home Design/Build at Yestermorrow Design/Build School, which was in its second year. Jersey Devil's practice returned, but Steve continued to teach, leading design/build studios across the country and finally landing permanently at the University of Washington in 1990.

That same year, on the other side of the continent, John began teaching at Yestermorrow. He opened this class, as he would each summer, by making a large-scale drawing of the words *design/build*. A hexagonal gazebo was completed nine days later. In the class photo, as the last wood shingles are nailed into place, ten students radiate satisfaction from the dappled shadows of their last afternoon work session.

Jim says that teaching is an opportunity to incorporate many years of experience into conversations with students, clients, and other educators. Teaching, particularly with design/build, frames a return to fundamentals. He has always been a natural at teaching—someone whose patience and rigor both affirm and challenge those working around him. But his introduction to formalized teaching came relatively late. It was on Jim's fiftieth birthday that one of Jersey Devil's clients asked him what the next decades would bring. Had he considered teaching? The following winter in 2000, Jim joined Steve and former University of Washington professor Sergio Palleroni for the school's Mexico Design/Build program. **Figs. 25–26** Three years later he was invited to teach the Home Design/Build course at Yestermorrow.

Design/build is reactive. Steve, Jim, and John teach students to react to site, program, and each other, and this dynamic learning process moves in two directions. Holding materials in hand elicits reactions: "Wow, that 2x8 is

Fig. 25 Biblioteca Pública Municipal Juana de Asbaje y Ramirez, Colonia Joya de Agua, Juitepec, Morelos, Mexico, University of Washington Design/Build Mexico, 2001.

Fig. 26 Biblioteca Pública Municipal under construction. Teaching refines how the designer/builder/practitioner makes things, and Jim finds that teaching is a way to continue learning. The Mexico projects introduced him to masonry, brickwork, and other building systems he had not used much in previous work. Each project requires innovation—pedagogically and materially, just as foreign locales challenge teacher and student alike with a new set of practices, resources, and experiences.

Fig. 27 El Centro De La Raza outdoor classrooms and community circle, Santos Rodriguez Memorial Park, Seattle, Washington, 2011.

Fig. 28 Interior of Arboretum Sunhouse, Washington State Arboretum, 2005.

heavier than I thought!" "How many of us will it take to move that component we prefabricated?" "The 2x4's depth fits my grip, and I can feel the slight curve—the 'cupping'—of this particular board's edge."

And in confronting situations, reactivity also brings student initiative: How do we solve this problem? How will our collaboration work? How does our work relate to the community's goals? Design/build provokes students' resourcefulness while taking stock of resources. "Me" becomes "us," and we soon realize that we must work together to complete our project. This collaboration is not just among each other but also with the broader community, and it ties back to the actual process of making. Speaking with Jersey Devil's members now reminds us of the way today's most pressing questions for architecture and design can be linked to how things are made.

GROUNDWORK

Each design/build project has three distinct but overlapping phases: preplanning before the project starts; then its day-to-day and week-to-week activities, which are often delimited by the studio's term; followed by final postproject activities. Focusing on the initial phase, this chapter looks at all the plans and considerations that lead up to the first day of design/build studio. How do you choose a project? How and when does design/build fit with other coursework? What preparation is necessary to set up the project? Two frameworks underlie this groundwork: design/build's placement within an overall curriculum, and the more particular goals of an individual project, which define the "why" of the project.

WHY DESIGN/BUILD?

The rationale for design/build studios is unique in its shared goals inside and outside the institution. Collaboration, communication, and construction infuse objectives for curriculum and community alike. Community service suggests a line extending outward from the institution, but feedback in this process means influences can work the other way as well. Communities affect those offering service. Steve recalls how Rural Studio's Sambo Mockbee said that students were "snake bit": though they might not immediately know the whole significance of what they had learned, their experience stays with them—as a kind of benign venom—and might indeed inspire them in the future. Design/build projects transform values, which in turn inform how people continue to design and build. **Fig. 01**

From an institutional and curricular perspective, design/build offers two related tracks: simple beginnings and complex syntheses. Its process asks students to bring together all that they have previously learned—conceiving design schemes, developing designs, working in groups, crafting models, presenting to reviewers (now clients), calculating loads, choosing materials, estimating costs, detailing joints, and even finishing a project. At the same time, it brings students back to the foundational elements of shelter and the root meaning of architecture: What do we design? Why do we build? For whom? Where is the appropriate place? How do we build? Constraints of time and skill factor into this return to basics, but the interaction—we might even say complicity—of design and build truly drives this refinement.

Identifying need—whether in terms of clients' intentions, resources, or infrastructure—plays into a design/build project's rationale. The return to basics in pedagogy fits well with the focus on necessities in a community. Design/build's flexible delivery methods, along with its student resources, allow for the undertaking of projects that might otherwise languish in bureaucratic logistics, fall between mission statements, or just not garner attention from civic organizations. Contributions of student labor and instructors' expertise help realize underfunded projects. Design/build's often unconventional project types might also not characteristically find their way into design school curriculum. Design/build consequently fills gaps of pedagogy and community attention. **Fig. 02**

Fig. 01 Students and members of the community enjoy the roasting pit to celebrate a project at Danny Woo Community Garden, 1990. Projects like this set up a long-term relationship between Steve's Neighborhood Design/Build Studio and Seattle's International District.

Fig. 02 Mobile Farmstand ("veggie wagon") for Shelburne Farms, Yestermorrow, 2007.

DESIGN/BUILD STUDIO OBJECTIVES

(a synthesis of goals from studios led by Jim, Steve, and John)

→ To foster a collaborative and consensus-driven design experience

→ To teach the value of collaborative thinking and understanding through building

→ To learn how knowledge of building expands our knowledge of design

→ To propose, discuss, revise, and edit design ideas through drawing and models to arrive at a collective design for construction

→ To integrate technology into design studio

→ To focus on issues of sustainability, accessibility, contextual fit, permanence, comfort, and beauty among other considerations

→ To develop communication skills in all media and situations, including building techniques that integrate concepts with methods of construction

→ To understand questions of tolerances and finished building attributes difficult to comprehend any other way

→ To redefine values and develop community service commitment

→ To empower students by broadening their experience and skills

→ To provide students with a range of roles in the design/build process to help them in future life choices

CURRICULUM

Inside and outside the studio. On campus and in the community. In the shop and on the jobsite. Design/build resides in a unique curricular space, a forum to teach at the intersection of *how* and *why*. Design process connects with methods of construction, while work in the university meets with its social, cultural, and even political implications. Design/build is not simply service learning nor merely designing and constructing; it teaches what Steve calls the "logic and poetics" of construction.

Design/build studios have the potential to relate to structures as well as materials and methods coursework. After the completion of a design/build studio, students have noted how they now "see" what those courses taught. And design/build does allow students to apply principles and techniques they have learned in previous classes, meshing well with the potential for design school curricula to provide direct and indirect links between studios and related coursework.

In some cases, a materials and methods course might lean toward design/build. Steve's work at the University of Washington carries on a tradition started in the 1970s by Andy Vanags and Barry Onouye, who linked their spring-quarter design/build playground studio to materials and structures

The best way to teach the logic and poetics of construction is to build. [Steve]

classes, which also included hands-on exercises in the school's wood and metal shop. At Ball State in the 1980s and '90s, Steve and John led hands-on materials seminars and studios that mixed design components with materials and methods curriculum. Students explored wood in a project using a sheet of plywood, metal in the design of an outdoor light fixture, concrete with a place marker cast from a 60-pound bag of ready mix, and a mixed-material project that addressed the flow and containment of water.

Fig. 03 School and plaza at Amun Shea, Perquin, El Salvador, MIT Department of Architecture design/build, 2009.

Fig. 04 Brickwork for plaza at Amun Shea, Perquin, El Salvador, MIT Department of Architecture design/build, 2009.

Fig. 05 School and plaza at Amun Shea, Perquin, El Salvador, MIT Department of Architecture design/build, 2009.

Design/build studios also offer opportunities for crossing disciplines. Steve's course attracts the college's dual-degree students who are enrolled in both architecture and construction management. Crossover also occurs with landscape architecture, planning, and real estate students. Jim's El Salvador project focused on the development of a plaza, allowing students to explore how landscape relates to buildings. **Figs. 03–05** And John's Yestermorrow course always brings in a diverse group, some with architecture backgrounds but many without, ranging from "high school students to retirees."

In the curriculum sequence, the course typically occurs in the final semester of undergraduate work and the second or third years of graduate study. Many programs have positioned their design/build studios to satisfy the sustainability criteria of the National Architectural Accrediting Board (NAAB), but that will likely change with the newest version of accreditation conditions. [see sidebar] At the University of Washington, Steve's design/build studio is among the courses—such as furniture and fab lab studios—that provide hands-on opportunities in the final quarter of the undergraduate sequence. For graduate students, his design/build option meets the college's sustainability requirement, and the studio's projects have served as examples of sustainability for previous NAAB reviews.

RELATION OF NAAB CONDITIONS FOR ACCREDITATION (2014) TO DESIGN/BUILD PEDAGOGY:

NAAB accredits professional degree programs in architecture. In the 2009 version of its Conditions for Accreditation, sustainability defined an entire category of student performance criteria with section 3 of educational realm B: "Ability to design projects that optimize, conserve, or reuse natural and built resources, provide healthful environments for occupants/users, and reduce the environmental impacts of building construction and operations on future generations through means such as carbon-neutral design, bioclimatic design, and energy efficiency."

In the 2014 revision, effective for 2016 accreditation visits, sustainability no longer defines its own category, potentially dispersing design/build's place within the student performance criteria. Although the idea of integrated project delivery (which relates to design/build) remains in the most recent revision, 2009's realm B "Integrated Building Practices" has become "Integrated Architectural Solutions" in 2014's realm C. Also, Collaboration and Community and Social Responsibility have been removed as secondary criteria in realm C. They are now included as a part of the "Defining Perspectives" for architecture programs.

For many years after Jersey Devil's time at Princeton, Leon Barth taught the lab component of the building systems course, which I took as an undergraduate architecture student. **Fig. 06** Once a week we laid up concrete blocks, framed stud walls, and fastened sheathing. The most dramatic endeavor was the brick arch with tension bars across the bottom. When it was completed, we removed the wooden forms and loaded the arch with blocks until it failed. In addition to these shorter exercises, we built a house throughout the semester in the glass cube attached to the lab's eastern end. Our poured concrete footings with block foundation set up the structure's 12-by-17-foot layout. As the fall semester progressed, the space grew colder but our rising confidence with the building process kept us busy, adding stucco on the interior sheathing and board-and-batten siding on the exterior, all of which was covered by an asphalt-shingled shed roof. Looking back, I know that this experience charted my own course of designing and building.

Fig. 06 Leon Barth teaching a lesson on bricklaying in the Architectural Lab at Princeton, 1992. The class completed an arch that was then tested to failure.

KEYSTONE

Capstone studios pull together all the material that has been previously covered in the curriculum. Comprehensive to the point of being terminal. Design/build studios work well as courses to integrate multiple learning outcomes, but even then they are more like thresholds and other connecting blocks. They serve as keystones rather than capstones. While the latter might be the last stone placed, the former is so integrated—as with an arch's keystone—that it is essential for the construction's stability. Design/build studios, as keystone courses, lock together the diverse elements of design pedagogy.

When I asked whether design/build studios are capstone courses, Jim said they would be his and Steve's "tombstone courses." Morbid humor aside, his response suggests that these studios are as much about the process as they are about the outcome. With design/build's substantial learning curve, the preparation, vigilance, and sheer time commitment that design/build demands can exhaust even the most experienced educator. And from the students' perspective, it is a threshold course that has one footing in core design curriculum and another in the many directions postgraduation life might take. Just as Jim, Steve, and John have spent their lives designing and building—and, as Jim suggests, will probably continue to do this until the end—design/build students develop new skills and the confidence to use them, all of which will continue to grow.

While not a capstone in the traditional sense, design/build does, for some students, mark a culmination of their academic careers. When design/build education is placed at the end of undergraduate coursework, it combines with a return to the basics and offers new experiences and perspectives at a moment when students may be feeling a redundancy in studio projects and associated work. It is invariably a moment for students to reflect—students have described the experience as a time to revisit concepts and techniques

Fig. 07 Firewood and garden shed, Huntington, Vermont, 2011.

they encountered in early design studios. First marks on a drawing, basic volumes, and simple connections return to significance and come into contact with building skills and community involvement. **Fig. 07** Essential design questions bring many students full circle.

LOCAL VS. GLOBAL

Design/build studios range from those that are local to the school's community to those that travel and work internationally. There are advantages and complexities to each. Steve believes programs that design and build close to home benefit from being "rooted in place"; as "active, productive members of their communities," such programs "build credibility with each project and benefit from past experiences, contacts, and reputation." When I visit Steve in Seattle, a half-day tour allows us to see more than a dozen projects he has completed with design/build studios, all of which serve as lessons for students and work samples for prospective clients. Local projects can employ "more sophisticated tools" and typically have ready access to shop facilities. **Fig. 08** Steve also reminds students that there are "plenty of problems at home" and they might be driving by "folks living in boxes on our way to the airport to fly off to another continent's project"—not to mention the embodied energy of an international project's extended reach.

On the other hand, international projects offer expanded horizons and cultural exchanges that local work might lack. Experiences abroad can be immersive. Jim notes that "you're living the whole design and build process," and these challenges can prove rewarding and life changing. **Fig. 09** Building with what is available opens students to vernacular crafts, new modes of production, and deep connections with previously unfamiliar places and ways of life. Simple technologies can be very effective in communities separated from development and opportunity.

A global version of their practice's itinerary, Jim and Steve's studios have designed and built from Africa to India, Cambodia to El Salvador, and Finland to Cuba. **Figs. 10–12** Jim prefers international projects:

"I like the challenge of working quickly and integrating the design ideas with what's culturally going on around you. A lot of things have to be assimilated in a short amount of time—the local building practice and budget, and the basics of shelter, such as water catchment, energy efficiency, and indigenous materials."

Long-term presence in foreign communities further augments linkages between culture and the design process. Over a period of ten years, University of Washington's Mexico Design/Build—with the involvement of Steve and Jim along with Sergio Palleroni, who now directs the Center for Public Interest Design at Portland State University—allowed for deep connections to the place with a dormitory and studio, a large set of tools, local contacts, and community respect. **Fig. 13**

Fig. 08 Steve has worked at Danny Woo Community Garden in Seattle's International District since 1990.

Fig. 09 Maternity Clinic Laundry Station, Perquin, El Salvador, MIT design/build, 2008. Jim's series of projects in El Salvador provided a background for the process of assimilation he describes.

Fig. 10 Arbor Loo Composting Toilet, Ghana, Africa, Miami University design/build, 2003. What has also been called "appropriate technology" is also "necessary technology" in the way that a foreign context requires design/build studios to return to basics, often with low-tech, but no less effective, solutions.

Fig. 11 Marketplace, Ghana, Africa, Miami University design/build, 2003.

Fig. 12 Urban Organic Agricultural Center, University of Washington design/build, Havana, Cuba, 2001.

Fig. 13 Escuela San Lucas: Elementary School Buildings, Colonia San Lucas, Tejalpa, Morelos, Mexico, 1995–97.

SCOPE

Jim's advice for small and simple projects targets the elemental scope of design/build work. Certain building types lend themselves to these criteria: pavilions, playgrounds, gardens, composting bathrooms, bus stops, and trailheads, for example, perform simple functions and often do not require extensive mechanical or environmental systems. [see "Type"] Limiting scope reduces the amount of work necessary to complete the project and at the same time allows room to play with variations on building typologies that can offer unique learning experiences.

By the same token, some projects can be too small. With the design and construction of a bike trailer, I learned that very small structures can make collaborative work difficult when no more than one or two students can actually work on it at the same time. More frequently, it is the tendency to expand projects—from small to large and from simple to complex—that threatens a project's success. **Figs. 14–16**

"**Keep it small, keep it simple.**" [Jim]

SCOPE CREEP

Scope creep is the impulse to increase a project's size and the intricacies of its construction. By extension, increases in time, work, and expense result from these changes, which come from many sources: Clients might ask for additions to program and space; for many students, design/build is their first experience with built work, and their enthusiasm packs this single project with multiple ideas; and instructors, as facilitators and advocates, can be equally sympathetic to the aspirations of both clients and students—ambitions that tend to expand a project's complexity. But Steve emphasizes the need for

Fig. 14 Mobile Writers' Studio, Shelburne, Vermont, Public Interest Design/Build at Yestermorrow, 2006.

Figs. 15–16 At Guara Ki, the simple, basic solution extends to low-tech processes—like humans hand-pumping water into small roof-level holding tanks for showers and the day's water supply (one tank holds cold water and the other solar-heated water).

focus: "Pretty soon, you figure out that you're not going to spend time custom building every single detail and you need to pick the heavy hits, the really good ones. Focus on that." In the design phase, he is known to offer frequent "reality checks" to student proposals. Scope is related to the definition of the problem and the main objectives of the project. Avoiding scope creep yields what Steve describes as a simpler, more clearly defined architecture and leads to a "legible solution" rather than a "whole bunch of ideas."

TIME

Jim and Steve link the scope of Yestermorrow's annual project to what can be constructed in two weeks, and Jim furthermore gauges what he can do in sixteen weeks at the University of Miami by the Yestermorrow studio's accomplishments over its two-week period. Yestermorrow students log at least nine hours each day, the equivalent of three three-hour studio sessions or two four-and-half-hour studios each week at Miami. These separate sessions also incur three times the effort in unrolling and then packing up tools. Working with a larger number of students does not necessarily yield greater efficiency. As Jim notes, even if you have a lot of students, you are still limited by class schedules and rhythms of the construction process. Enrolling more students requires more logistics to distribute tasks, manage work, and apportion tools. Only so many people can share a circular saw, and there may not always be enough charged cordless drills or sufficient space to use them when fastening components.

Scope is intimately connected to time and schedule." [Jim]

Design/build takes time, and schedules of education and construction sometimes conflict with one another. "I warn everybody up front we are all going to hold up the class at some point or another." John further summarizes the paradoxes of teaching and building: "There's the educational goal to allow the students opportunities to do something they've never done before that is at odds with efficiency and productivity." Students need time to learn. So, in a certain sense, design/build is an exercise in slowness—not rushing for the sake of safety and pacing yourself for the sake of learning objectives.

SIZE

Bill Bialosky, who teaches with Jim and Steve at Yestermorrow, likes to say that if the studio's twelve or so students joined hands and spread out, they would create the size parameters of what they can effectively build in two weeks. To gauge what size project can be completed in time and on budget, Jim notes some baseline dimensions determined by vehicular transport requirements: "Our projects usually aren't any longer than twenty feet or any wider than eight and a half feet or any taller than ten feet." With Yestermorrow's projects, a main concern is component size. Instructors consider what can be transported from the school's workshop down the road to the particular site, so scope and size are also functions of mobility. **Figs. 17–18**

Fig. 17 Story Time Pavilion for Magic Mountain Daycare, South Royalton, Vermont, Yestermorrow's Community Design/Build, 1996.

Fig. 18 Transporting the Story Time Pavilion.

TYPES OF DESIGN/ BUILD PROJECTS IN JIM, JOHN, AND STEVE'S STUDIOS

Bike storage
Park bench
Outdoor seating areas
Composting toilet
Garden structures
General storage shed
Equipment shed
Tool storage shed
Garden shed
Chicken shed
Playground structure
Gazebo
Gathering space
Outdoor stairway
Living fence

Fruit stand
Bus stop
Trailheads and trail
    shelters
Orchid pavilion
Garden pavilion
Waiting shelter
Porch
Mobile kitchen
Sanitary facility
Playground
Performance and play
    stage
Pedestrian bridge
Outdoor classroom
Community garden
Eco-tent
Greenhouse (lath house,
    sun house)

Deck and facade
    remodel
Supershed
Marketplace
Visitor pavilion and
    laundry station
School and plaza
Rural kitchen
Solar kitchen
Agricultural center
Library remodel
Library
Community center
School
Pavilion dormitory

TYPE

From community gardens to rural kitchens, supersheds to composting toilets, and fences to facades, Jim, Steve, and John's projects enlist a wide programmatic range while also offering scalar consistency. Many of these building types are open-air and provide direct links between climate and the human body. Similarly, most of the projects are public, linking the interventions to the wider population just as design/build connects students with the broader community.

Project types also depend on the client. The range of Steve's projects can be attributed to his partnerships with Inter*im Community Development Association, the Lao Highlands Association, Wellspring Family Services, and many other nonprofit groups. For their design/build studio projects, Jim and University of Miami professor Rocco Ceo have found a diverse selection from the range of educational, environmental, and agricultural nonprofit outfits and organizations in South Florida. And John's recent series of outbuildings and sheds demonstrates the rich learning experiences in the construction of utilitarian structures.

BUDGET

Scope is also determined by budget. Since students provide labor, Jim points out that "if you don't get complex—if it's not a kitchen or a bathroom with lots of plumbing—it's lumber that takes up most of the budget." On Steve and Jim's Yestermorrow projects, roof material and fasteners comprise a major expense. With the latter, the outdoor screws that make up the primary connection method are costlier than nails, and cordless drills require more maintenance than hammers.

For Steve's Neighborhood Design/Build Studio, the minimum budget for projects in the last ten years has been $10,000—earlier projects were cheaper. Jim and Rocco's projects at the University of Miami have ranged from $5,000 to two or three times that. At Yestermorrow, in their collaboration on the Public Interest Design/Build studio, they have rarely had more than a few thousand dollars. For these projects, locally milled, rough-sawn timber comes to them at a fraction of the cost of lumberyards. **Fig. 19** Materials for John's garden shed projects at Yestermorrow typically cost about $2,400, based on $30 per square foot for an eighty-square-foot project. John sees the shed construction as a good lesson for the class, a tangible and legible indication of how much material goes into a relatively small building. As he notes, even though the materials can all fit in a pickup truck, "It's still more than a thousand dollars."

Materials are the main cost. [Jim]

Fig. 19 Baird's Mill in Waitsfield, Vermont, near Yestermorrow Design/Build School.

Tight budgets are useful constraints that prepare students for the realities of professional practice and building construction, but for Steve limited funding can also "affect every decision and rule out many really good options, both in terms of design and fabrication." The Urban Farm Supershed project had the Neighborhood Design/Build Studio's tightest budget—even with $11,000, the structure's scale and complexity required material innovations along with donations of additional materials for completion.

There are pros and cons to bigger budgets. Sometimes, as Jim notes, when "greater funds allow for greater scope," an expanded budget can foster greater complexity, which "isn't necessarily a good thing." Jim's Mobile PermaKitchen project included the retrofit of a travel trailer, movable panels, spring-loaded canopies, photovoltaic panels, a custom-built solar hot water heater, a back up propane generator, and all the components to teach food preparation—appliances, counters, and storage. To date, the largest budget for Steve's Neighborhood Design/Build Studio was 2014's Danny Woo Neighborhood Cookery, which cost $30,000 but was still 25 percent below the $40,000 allowed for the project. Steve notes that this cushion provided flexibility to bill for overhead, meet the challenges of the project's details and moving parts, and hire a project manager who served as a liaison with city administration and design review boards.

And saving money must be balanced with saving time. At Yestermorrow, the rough lumber, donated in each of the four projects for Shelburne Farms, requires a few extra days for more extensive processing—straightening, ripping, and planing—to address the lack of material uniformity. Steve and Jim have calculated that the lumber required for a typical Yestermorrow project would cost $3,500 if it came from the local building supply company.

BUDGETS FOR SELECTED DESIGN/ BUILD PROJECTS

(note that these are estimates and primarily account for materials)

← Steve and Jim's Trailhead project at Yestermorrow
(2008)
$2,000

John's typical garden shed at Yestermorrow
(2009)
$2,400

Pavilion and Work Areas at Highland Gardens
(1998)
$2,500

Outdoor classroom
(Yestermorrow, 2014)
$3,500

Amun Shea Plaza, Perquin, El Salvador
(2009)
$5,000

Motes Orchid Pavilion
(2009)
$5,000

Rural Kitchen, Siem
Reap, Cambodia
(2010)
$6,000

Play Courts at
Experimental
Education Unit
(1995)
$7,000

← Coffee Kiosk
(2014)
$8,450

Guara Ki Bathhouse
(2013)
$8,000

Play Court for infants
 and toddlers
(1997)
$11,000

Danny Woo stairs and
accessible gardens
(1996)
$12,000

Room for a Forest
(2013)
$13,550

Everglades Eco-Tent
(2012)
$17,000

Danny Woo neighborhood
cookery
(2014)
$30,000

FUNDING

The basic model is that clients cover material costs while the class delivers a design with labor for construction services. For studio projects, Steve works to raise funds with the clients, which are typically nonprofits and eligible for grants and tax-deductible donations. Steve writes a letter of support to accompany the submissions and works with clients to apply for these grants and make the case for the design/build studio's effectiveness. In the Neighborhood Design/Build Studio's work, Seattle's Department of Neighborhoods provides an ideal resource for matching funds toward projects with short turnaround times, particularly through the Small and Simple Projects Funds program. The department also matches community-generated—resources such as material donations, labor, donated professional services, and client contributions—with cash. And in funding applications, design/build studios can present a strong case with a large number of volunteer hours, the sheer numbers of the class's labor force compensating for what it might lack in terms of skill. In Steve's studio, sixteen (and sometimes as many as eighteen) students plus three instructors, working twenty hours per week for eleven weeks, totals 4,180 volunteer hours. **Fig. 20**

Fig. 20 Students working on the Children's Garden Neighborhood Cookery, 2014.

FUND-RAISING

Raising funds for design/build projects is challenging. Potential sources include local and regional businesses, foundations, and the academic institution itself. Students help solicit donations and approach prospective donors once the studio has a design scheme with selected materials. Steve and Jim provide additional letters of support, and donors will need evidence of tax-exempt status along with state (if applicable) and federal identification numbers.

POTENTIAL FUNDING SOURCES:

City agencies
Architecture firms
Construction companies
Engineering firms
Hardware stores
Building material stores and suppliers
Etching companies (for plaques)
Community development associations
Private donors and foundations
Universities and colleges (Dean's Office)
Fastener companies
Solar energy companies
Neighborhood reinvestment corporations
Reprographic companies
Plant societies (for community gardens)
Steel fabricators
Electric and other utility companies
Housing associations
University alumni

Typically, logistics of tax-exempt status will best be handled through a nonprofit client with 501(c)(3) status. For Steve's projects, donations to the University of Washington Foundation are tax deductible, and in other cases it is possible to work through a university system claiming tax-exempt status as a corporation "operated exclusively for educational, research, and public service."

At the University of Miami, Jim and Rocco work with a development officer to solicit contributions from alumni and other benefactors. These funds help the design/build studio acquire and maintain tools, pay for visiting faculty salaries, and support future plans for a separate design/build building. Steve fund-raises for his program through contacts with local design/build companies, family foundations, and alumni of the university and the studio itself. The Neighborhood Design/Build Studio's gift fund supports tools, computers, publications, work-study students, and trips to lectures and conferences to present studio work.

Understood as integral to the studio, fund-raising can become a dynamic part of the design/build process. When students seek donations, they engage themselves with the community, and the endeavor can also strengthen the studio group with the shared goals, logistics, and clear objectives required when raising money. Much can be accomplished in the first weeks of a studio, but students must have time—and, in many cases, transportation—to pursue donors. Though face-to-face meetings are often most effective, students also make phone calls and draft donation request letters to fax or email to potential donors.

Crafting a letter refines how students perceive and communicate project goals. To write a convincing 100-word project statement to someone unfamiliar with the studio in particular and design/build in general is to clarify objectives and to extend the reach of an educational process that is oftentimes closed off from community interaction. Such communications mirror how students, as design professionals, will later convey ideas to clients and broader communities.

Crowdfunding platforms can also build and extend community. Kickstarter, Facebook, and RocketHub, among others, extend the pool of donors beyond a locale and allow friends, family, and advocates to play a part in the project from a distance. Even as it remains virtual, this social medium augments the participatory spirit of design/build. In contrast to many crowdfunding requests that are more speculative and often less tangible, design/build projects are readily visualized and typically already in process, so that potential crowd-funders can easily see where their donations will go.

ENROLLMENT

Steve and Jim identify twelve as the ideal number of students in a design/build studio. In Steve's Neighborhood Design/Build Studio, pressures on class size have increased enrollment to sixteen and more recently to eighteen. More students require increased supervision, and the studio typically has two instructors—Steve and Jake LaBarre—as well as a work-study student who has previously taken the course and can assist with studio activities. As Steve notes, larger numbers also make the "consensus design process more difficult and cumbersome." Yestermorrow's enrollment has ranged from ten to fourteen—a studio of ten is the minimum for financial viability but allows students to take on more varied roles; fourteen adds organizational complexity and pushes the limit of what the small-scale project can sustain, but does result in a faster pace.

The courses Jim and Steve teach are vertical studios, enrolling both undergraduate and graduate students. At the University of Miami, the design/build studio is open to fourth-year seniors and graduate students. At the University of Washington, seniors in their final quarter join the studio with graduate students who are either in the first of two years or in the second year of the three-year master of architecture program. The mix of younger with older students provides a range of unique perspectives, even if only divided by a few years of experience.

Both programs use a selection process to bring in students who want to learn design/build and to keep the enrollment at an appropriate number. After instructors have presented the semester's studio options at the University of Miami, students rank their choices, which are further narrowed by seniority and grade point average. At the University of Washington, Steve uses an application process in which students submit resumes, letters of interest, and portfolios; and he tries to put together a studio divided evenly in terms of graduate and undergraduate applicants. Despite this mix, design/build's educational process is an equalizer that brings different experiences and skill sets together for a common goal.

PREPLANNING
PROJECT

The design/build project typically starts at least six months in advance of its initiation in class. Such preplanning allows adequate time to visit potential sites and develop the program with the client. Establishing a preferred location on the site saves time by reducing design decisions during the first couple of weeks, particularly if the project is on a large public site that can present multiple options. Project selection takes into account scope, size, timeline, budget, schedule, and client availability. It is also a good idea to have a backup plan because projects can fall through, and, as Steve says, "The studio dates are fixed!" **Figs. 21–23**

With international projects, preplanning is often extended. For Auroville's pavilion, Jim and Steve traveled to India in September 2001 to present students' preliminary design proposals. Even though the clients asked for a redesign, there was enough time to review new schemes before the studio began in the following spring, and students were building by the second week. Preplanning for projects abroad might also include a predeparture course—when students enrolled in the Global Community Studio at the University of Washington, they took a preparatory seminar for global studies that provided background for cross-cultural exchange.

One project might open up possibilities for many more. Steve's involvement with Danny Woo Community Garden began with a garden toolshed designed and built as an independent study. Eighty square feet led to more than an acre of design/build work in a series of projects spanning more than two decades. These larger projects might take a phased approach when the scope of work exceeds what can be accomplished in one school term. In such cases, it is essential for each phase to have its own unique design problem so that students in a second or third phase of the broader project are not left merely to complete a previous studio's scheme. The Neighborhood Design/Build Studio used a phased approach for Bradner Gardens Park, T. T. Minor Elementary School, the Experimental Education Unit play spaces, and Danny Woo Community Garden. At Bradner, a central pavilion followed earlier phases that included a footbridge and trellis components; and T. T. Minor's trellis with equipment sheds preceded a performance and play stage. Work at Danny Woo continues today in a series of installments. **Figs. 24–28**

" **I try to line up projects as far in advance as possible, but don't get nervous until the fall before the spring studio.**" [Steve]

Fig. 21 Changes of plan sometimes do occur in the middle of a design/build studio term. Steve's 2008 NDBS project shifted from Seattle Tilth to the Lao Highlands Association. Layout of trusses in week ten for Lao Highlands project.

Fig. 22 Setting frames and trusses for Lao Highlands project.

Fig. 23 Completed project for Lao Highlands, 2008.

Fig. 24 Trellis at Bradner Gardens design/build project, 1999.

Fig. 25 Footbridge at Bradner Gardens, 1999.

Fig. 26 Eastern entry built in phase one (1999) and pavilion (in the background) built in phase two at Bradner Gardens (2000).

Fig. 27 Pavilion at Bradner Gardens, 2000.

SITE

After selecting the type of project and the place, another level of decision making identifies a particular site. Jim, along with teaching assistants, spent a week of preplanning in Cambodia to establish the general site location for the studio. This in-country preparation allowed for a process of discovery for understanding the context, its local histories and building traditions, and also included research about logistics of transportation, translation, materials, local producers, and seasonal climates.

Fig. 28 Trellis and equipment sheds at T. T. Minor Elementary School, 2001.

Sites must also sometimes be chosen on the fly. For the 2009 MIT project in El Salvador, Jim and a vanguard of students arrived to prepare for the studio project to design and build a stage and amphitheater on a site in a refugee community, only to find that the client did not own the land. With the students' arrival imminent, Jim talked with Ron Brenneman, past collaborator and founder of the Amun Shea elementary school, who suggested that the group address the entry space in front of the two recently constructed classrooms at the school. This rapid shift of site afforded the studio a project that could engage landscape elements and provide a useful plaza space between the buildings. **Fig. 29**

Fig. 29 School and Plaza at Amun Shea, Perquin, El Salvador, MIT Department of Architecture design/build, 2009.

CLIENT

Clients are an integral part of the design/build studio. And, often, they will find you. In Jim's case for the Eco-Tent project, the Parks Department visited the University of Miami Architecture Department to look for interns who might be interested in helping with projects, and Rocco Ceo saw it as an opportunity for a design/build project. **Fig. 30**

Fig. 30 Studio discussion with Everglades National Park rangers for the Eco-Tent, 2012.

Such coincidences can work, but fledgling programs must start somewhere, and Steve's first design/build studio at the University of Washington began on campus with the Stairway to Nowhere in 1988. The Stairway went somewhere, and, two years later, Leslie Morishita, who had recently completed the garden toolshed as her independent study with University of Washington faculty members, recruited Steve to lead a summer studio to design and build a pig roast pit and kiosks at Danny Woo Community Garden. Combined with Leslie's toolshed, this project set up an array of future work as a first link with Seattle's International District community.

Keeping in touch with previous clients yields follow-up work or generates leads for other projects. Steve's current studios often contribute time to maintain past projects—in 2008, when the studio switched clients from Seattle Tilth to Lao Highlands, students made repairs to the Stairway to Nowhere, and that reputation for repairs and upkeep instills confident references. Sergio Palleroni, who cofounded Design/Build Mexico with Steve at the University of Washington, has noted that the program's sustained presence in the community led to the eventual engagement and buy-in from the Ministry of Education for the Escuela Rosario Castellanos project. Steve has also found that former students are a good source for potential projects, whether they work for nonprofits, architecture firms, or local government. It doesn't hurt that an estimated 80 percent of University of Washington graduates stay in Seattle, and program graduates serve as ambassadors for future design/build work. Steve also attends community meetings, galas, and celebrations to keep a high profile in the nonprofit world. Steve's coteachers Damon Smith and Jake LaBarre have also brought in projects.

Design/build projects in schools typically engage clients to a greater degree than conventional architectural design practices in the profession tend to, and furthermore, some clients might take an active role throughout the process. Interactions between client and students can be a key part of the educational experience. And as a project develops, clients often see unexpected possibilities through conversations with the studio group and visits to the site. Mario Yanez, the client for the Guara Ki Bathhouse, shared his expertise with sustainable materials and challenged students to think about alternative materials. During the design review, Mario applauded the overall design but asked the students to consider alternative materials that were more renewable, while they also looked for ways to reduce the project's cost. Students replaced the copper gutter system with aluminum components and changed the wood specification to western red cedar certified by the Forest Stewardship Council. The design/build process offers a level of engagement and connectivity that often allows for changes to accommodate those new perspectives.

CODES AND BUILDING PERMITS

Many years ago Steve quipped that the only license he carried was a driver's license. The members of Jersey Devil possess experience that rivals any license, and in their own design/build projects they have been able to demonstrate this expertise, sometimes in formal presentations given to building departments. But for the rest of us, projects must navigate often complex bureaucratic and administrative processes. There are two sides: the credentials of those directing the design/build project and the codes of construction. Design/build projects fall into a regulated context for health, safety, and welfare, and the need for licensure and permits depends on the project's scope and location.

DO YOU NEED A PERMIT?

(from Seattle Department of Planning and Development's website)

You probably need a permit in Seattle if your project involves new or changed property uses or construction or alteration of a building—even if you can't see the alteration from the outside. Even if a permit is not required, your project must meet all code requirements and development standards. Some small projects do not need a permit. Unless you're in an environmentally critical area, the following projects usually don't require a permit:

Minor repairs or alterations

You don't need a permit for minor repairs or alterations that cost $4,000 or less in any six-month period. You need a permit for any work on load-bearing supports, changes to the building envelope, and work that reduces egress, light, ventilation, or fire resistance, no matter how small the project.

Miscellaneous work

These projects usually don't require a permit:

→ Patio and concrete slabs on the ground (on grade)
→ Painting or cleaning a building
→ Repointing a chimney
→ Installing kitchen cabinets
→ Paneling or other surface finishes over existing wall and ceiling systems
→ Insulating existing buildings
→ Abatement of hazardous materials
→ In-kind or similar replacement of or repair of deteriorated parts of a structure

Building and landscaping

You usually don't need a permit for:

→ A one-story detached accessory building, such as a greenhouse, tool or storage shed, playhouse, or similar building, if the projected roof area is less than 120 square feet and the building foundation is only a slab on the ground
→ Some retaining walls and rockeries that are not over four feet in height measured from the bottom of the footing to the top of the wall
→ Fences that are less than eight feet high and have no concrete or masonry elements higher than six feet
→ Arbors or other open-framed landscape structures that don't exceed 120 square feet in area

Platforms, walks, and driveways

You do not need a permit for these if they are less than eighteen inches above grade and not over a basement or other building story.

Fig. 31 Highland Gardens pavilion, Issaquah, Washington, 1998.

Fig. 32 Mobile PermaKitchen design/build project, 2010–11.

In Seattle Steve looks for projects that do not need permits. When required, "The permitting process is a good experience for students, just one we usually don't have time for" because of time pressures to complete projects in an eleven-week quarter. City code typically does not require permits for concrete slabs on grade, fences less than eight feet high, retaining walls four feet high or less, and small outbuildings like greenhouses, storage sheds, or playhouses. This stipulation has been a good fit for Steve's community garden projects that include arbors and "open-framed landscape structures" of modest floor area. **Fig. 31** Steve has also been able to construct a series of these smaller structures "connected by trellises or grouped together to form exterior spaces." Seattle's building department offers a subject to field inspection (STFI) permit, with a more streamlined application process, from which projects like the Room for a Forest have benefited.

Jim notes that his design/build studio cannot take on projects that require permits, because of the studio schedule and Miami-Dade County's extensive permitting process. Consequently, his studio chooses agricultural projects that typically remain outside this process, and they often put the project on wheels or skids so that its mobility exempts it from the limitations of site-built work. Both Guara Ki Bathhouse and the Mobile PermaKitchen were classified as mobile facilities. **Fig. 32** At Yestermorrow, the Public Interest Design/Build studio uses similar strategies, but most projects have not required permits under Vermont's relatively liberal building regulations. The Four Corners Bus Stop needed a permit because of its location and intensive public use, but the small-town accessibility of Warren, Vermont's one-person building department eased the process.

TOOLBOX

TOOLS

Using a tool is not merely a skill; it also carries implications for how to build and how to design. Tools link eye with hand, and sometimes, even for an experienced craftsperson, hammer to thumb. They also bind making to thinking and join the conceptual, technical, and physical—what John calls "forms of learning." The pedagogy of the tool links studio, jobsite, and workshop. With a knowledge of tools, problem solving can fold back into the design process and creativity will extend to how things are put together.

There are hand tools and power tools. Jersey Devil favors neither. There are tools for digital and manual fabrication. Design/build benefits from both. There are tools to organize a day's work, to structure an inclusive process, and to engage materials; there are tools that embrace the craftiness of crafting and act as expedients for moving a project along; there are tools for safety, for simplicity, and for fun—the design/build studio's toolbox includes not only implements you can hold but tactics you can watch, hear, and practice.

To inventory these tools is to imagine their many combinations—a block plane can ready cedar's grained surface for the orbital sander's gentle but insistent grind, a circular saw rips across a board whose corner is then eased by a hand-drawn rasp file, and wood chisels clean out what a jig saw cannot reach. Mock-ups and jigs translate tools of drafting to shop and site. Feedback inspires consensus, responds to materials, and ultimately splices design together with build. Play lightens the mood as it also anchors improvisation. Just don't expect to find the wood-stretcher in your toolbox.

Fig. 01 A fully equipped tool belt.

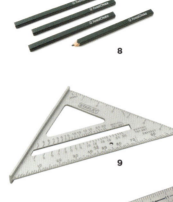

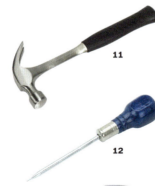

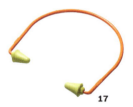

1

2

3

4

5

6

7

8

9

10

11

12

13

14

15

16

17

1	Crayons
2	Sharpies
3	Nail sets
4	Rasp file
5	Chalk line reel (chalk box)
6	Torpedo level (magnetic)
7	Utility knife
8	Pencils
9	Speed square
10	Combination square*
11	Claw hammer
12	Scratch awl
13	Measuring tape (25 feet)
14	Hammer holster
15	Gloves
16	Safety glasses
17	Ear protection

HANDS-ON

"Hands-on" is just that—putting your hands *on* what you are making. Hands-on means getting dirty, using tools, and literally touching what is being made. **Fig. 02** Many of those who come to design/build sign on because they want to use their hands, an act they equate to practical experience; or sometimes it's an opportunity to get outside the studio and the conventions of professional practice. Hands certainly grasp, measure, and touch. They offer the immediacy of implements, dimensions, and experiences. But, as a tool for involvement, hands-on goes deeper, raising awareness of body and materials, while it is also building community.

"*I always know where my hands are.*" [Jim]

Teaching the design/build student to use tools covers not only what the hand does—how to hold the tool, whether manually or electrically powered—but also what the rest of the body is doing. Jim is quick to point out that he is always mindful of where his hands are. Often surprised by how unaccustomed his students are to the physicality that is a part of construction, John teaches students "centering techniques" to position and balance themselves and "connect their legs to the ground." **Fig. 03** Demonstrations and supervised repetitive practice help students understand how tools are extensions of the hand while exposing them to Steve's idea that it is the whole body that accomplishes building. Overall body strength, not just hand strength, aligns and powers (but not overpowers) the drills and circular saws on the site. And such control of the tool leads to empowerment. **Fig. 04**

Fig. 02 Hands working on the Sunhouse project, Washington State Arboretum, 2005.

 *The try square ("try" for testing) is similar to the combination square but does not adjust its straight edge. Along with the squaring piece, attachments for these tools include the bevel protractor (right) and the centering head that draws radial lines through the center of a curved surface. Browsing a New Hampshire store's cheap tool bin,  Jersey Devil discovered a related tool: the J-square, which they used to lay out the purlins on the Helmet House rafters.

1

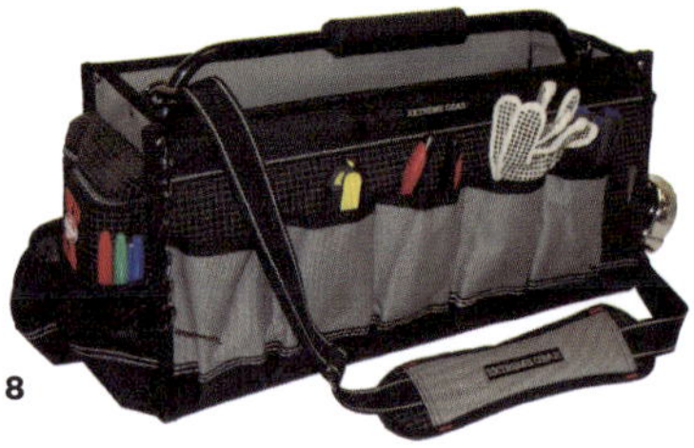

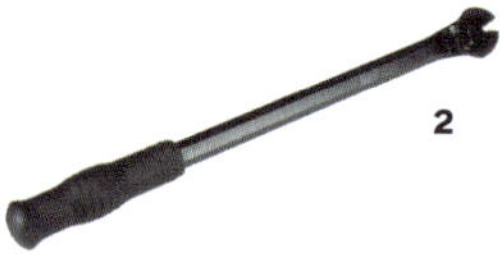

2

3

4

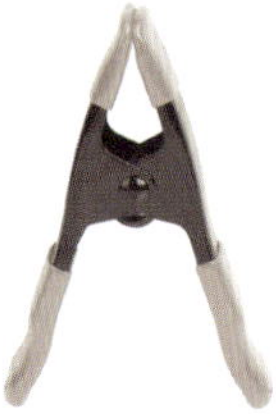

8

9

10a

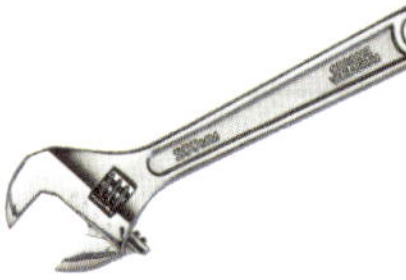

10b

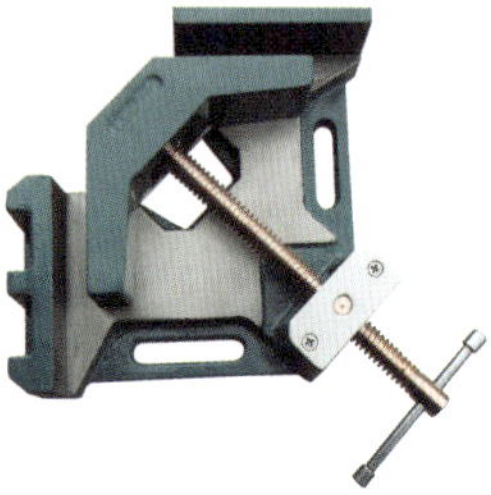

10c

5

11

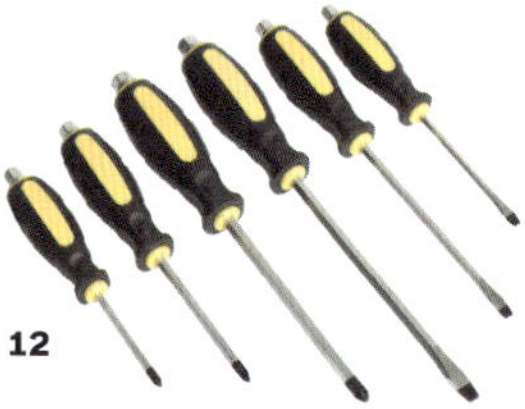

12

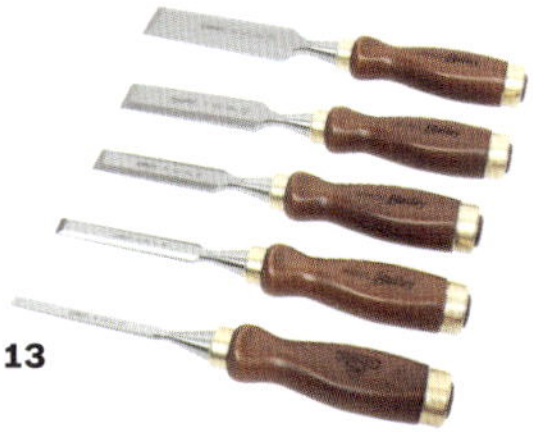

13

6

7

14

15

16

17

18

1   Adjustable wrench
2   Cat's paw (nail puller)
3   Flat pry bar
4   Angle bevel (T-bevel)
5   Framing square
6   Ripping bar
7   Lineman's pliers
8   Tool bag (soft)
9   Hand saws (pull stroke)
10   Clamps (a: spring,
       b: angle, and c: hand-
       screw)
11   Box-beam level (2 feet)
12   Screwdrivers
13   Wood chisels
14   Long tape (100 feet)
15   Plumb bob
16   Nylon string
17   Jack plane
18   Block plane
19   Wood-stretcher**
20   Sky hook**

John distributes this handout during the first meeting of his studio at Yestermorrow.

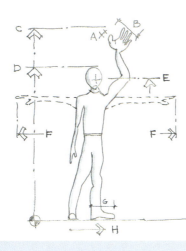

MY PERSONAL SCALE

A = THUMB WIDTH =

B = HAND SPAN =

C.1 = REACH (FLAT FOOTED) =

C.2 = REACH (TIP-TOES) =

D = HEIGHT =

E.1 = EYE HEIGHT (STANDING) =

E.2 = EYE HEIGHT (SITTING) =

F = WIDTH =

G = FOOT =

H = PACE =

The hand is itself a tool. So-called rules of thumb allow for quick measurements and further link body to design and construction. Thumbs are about one inch wide. Measuring across all five fingers tightly drawn typically yields four inches—a dimension conventionally identified as the "hand." Four fingers across the second knuckle amount to three inches—a distance sometimes confusingly referred to as the "palm." From the tip of your little finger to the tip of your thumb "spans" about nine inches. Hands come in different sizes, and each standard should be checked against your own digits, making for a personal—quite literally manual—toolbox of quick measurements. I know that the width of my own index finger near the tip is ¾" and the side of my pinkie measures ½". Other parts of the body also measure. Leonardo da Vinci's Vitruvian Man reminds us that extending both arms transfers our vertical height to a horizontal dimension. And further down, a foot (shod with shoe) is about a foot.

This close contact engages visual, tactile, and even olfactory senses, but other operations are also

** Fictional tools requested on the jobsite to fool novice builders. A wood-stretcher lengthens a board that has been cut too short. Sky hooks also do not exist. Novices or apprentices might be asked to retrieve such imaginary tools.

Fig. 03 Lifting columns for Children's Garden Cookery at Danny Woo Community Garden, 2014.

Fig. 04 Drilling a pole for the Everglades Eco-Tent project, 2012.

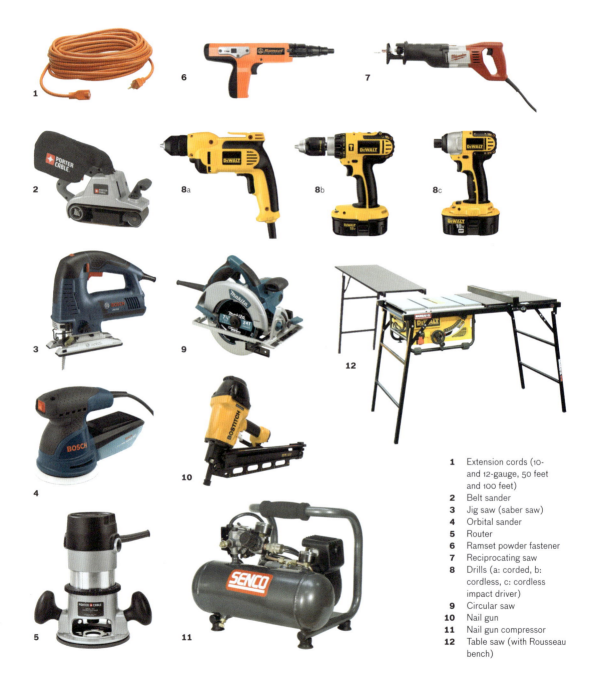

1 Extension cords (10- and 12-gauge, 50 feet and 100 feet)
2 Belt sander
3 Jig saw (saber saw)
4 Orbital sander
5 Router
6 Ramset powder fastener
7 Reciprocating saw
8 Drills (a: corded, b: cordless, c: cordless impact driver)
9 Circular saw
10 Nail gun
11 Nail gun compressor
12 Table saw (with Rousseau bench)

at work. Hands-on in design/build links students to materials and site and further connects students to each other. **Fig. 05** A hands-on approach allows students to produce what you will use for construction. When students mix concrete, they are actually making the material for the project. Wheelbarrow, hoe, shovel, and garden hose become root technologies, and though it doesn't get more basic, such a simple process involves all students. Hands-on can then foster teamwork and extend a project's community reach, reminiscent of a town's cooperation sandbagging for floods.

Fig. 05 Completing the assembly of Beacon Food Forest's modules, which have been lined up over the footing holes.

At the Danny Woo Community Garden in Seattle's International District, Steve's students hand mixed the equivalent of three truckloads of concrete. **Figs. 06–09** The process went something like this: unload sixty-pound bags of ready mix; pass them from person to person, then stack and store in a Mobile Mini (or other dry jobsite storage); drop bags in wheelbarrow (two at a time); roll to formwork, cut first bag with hoe blade; flip bag and pour into wheelbarrow; add water (not too much at a time) with a nozzled hose; stir first batch with a hoe (the kind with holes); mix to a soupy consistency (this is OK for the first batch to save energy); add the second bag; mix thoroughly until it feels (not tastes) like cookie dough; deliver to pour site, rolling the wheelbarrow if possible—if not, then buckets and shovels can do the work. The poured concrete formalized the community gardens, just as mixing it structured the hands-on process and teamwork among the design/builders.

This rudimentary and repetitive activity also links design/build students to size, scale, and quantity. How much does a bag of concrete weigh? How much (or how little) does its contents yield? Such questions link to another query, childlike in its simplicity but astute in its connection of material and project: How much concrete in a mixer truck? It's about ten cubic yards, easily filling more than one hundred wheelbarrows. That's three hundred trips for the students at Danny Woo. Doing relates such quantities to experience. When you lift a bag of concrete, you weigh a piece of a wall. When you and your crew raise a wall panel by hand, you become temporary braces, feeling the wall's tilt and the lateral forces at work, while also sensing the necessary teamwork and understanding that constructed spaces are vitally interconnected. **Figs. 10–11**

> **For concrete pours, we typically use the store-bought ready mix between 3,500 and 4,000 psi (compared to the 2,500 or 3,000 psi of footing concrete delivered by truck). The stronger ready mix accounts for home-owner types who might add too much water.** [Steve]

Fig. 06 Stacked bags of concrete, Danny Woo Community Garden, International District, Seattle, 2003.

Fig. 07 Unloading bags of concrete.

Fig. 08 Moving bags to the site.

Fig. 09 Concrete retaining walls at Danny Woo Community Garden.

Fig. 10 Students and instructors lift a 20-foot piece of formwork into place for Escuela San Lucas: Elementary School Buildings, 1995–97.

Fig. 11 Construction of the Armadillo Structure for Patch Adams' Gesundheit Institute: The Chrysalis, Yestermorrow Community Design/Build, 2004.

MATERIALS

Materials are active agents in the design/build process. There is a particular joy in touching, lifting, and placing the stuff buildings are made of. Dimension, weight, strength, aspect, appearance, and texture. Experiencing these qualities will affirm, contradict, and always challenge our preconceptions. Lift a 16-inch concrete block; grasp an 8-foot-long 2x4; wield the lightness of an aluminum channel while holding its finish (matte or polished) to the light; hold a piece of translucent polycarbonate up to the same light.

Materials for design/build can be hard to come by. Budgets are often limited, and turnaround times for orders can be tight. Local sourcing helps. At Yestermorrow, Jim and Steve often work with Shelburne Farms, which provides its own rough-sawn lumber—logged, milled, and air-dried on the farm. Dedicated storage spaces can offer long-term inventories of leftover materials and off-season donations. But in many cases, design/build relies on creative sourcing for its building materials. **Figs. 12–13**

Off-the-shelf components offer a reliable stock for construction components and opportunities to develop a project around the materials at hand. Yestermorrow's two-week schedule necessitates the use of readily available materials. For the Shelburne Farms composting toilet components, Jim, Steve, and Bill limited the students' design scheme to what they could find at Kenyon's Variety Store, a local hardware and agricultural supply store in Waitsfield, Vermont. **Fig. 14** Garbage cans, plumbing fixtures, and flexible tubing all evoked possible solutions and configurations. Just as he did in Jersey Devil projects, Jim encouraged students to think innovatively by challenging them to use materials in ways that differed from their planned functions.

"**Materials have a way of humbling designers unless the designer understands what the material can do.**" [John]

Fig. 12 Composting toilet structure for Shelburne Farms, 2013. At Yestermorrow, Jim and Steve often use locally sourced wood, but its roughness sometimes requires intensive processing and preparation.

Fig. 13 Four Corners bus shelter, East Warren, Vermont, 2002. Over time, the material takes on a rich weathered patina.

Fig. 14 Shelburne Farms Composting Toilet at Yestermorrow, 2012, with garbage can components. Jim's studio at the University of Miami further developed this composting system with the Guara Ki Bathhouse.

Fig. 15 Play structure with satellite dish roof at Verd-Mont Trailer Park, Waitsfield, Vermont, 2003. For this class, student Ben Cheney discovered the dish offered for free in the local *Nickel* paper. Like an inverted umbrella, it formed the rocket's translucent nose cone and protected kids from rain and sun.

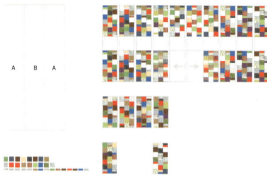

A B A

Fig. 16 Drawing of patchwork patterns for Wellspring Family Services Playhouse, 2009.

Fig. 17 Wellspring Family Services Playhouse and Living Fence, 2009.

Design/builders are bricoleurs, adapting materials for unintended uses and achieving goals of construction indirectly and by other unconventional means. For the bricoleur, an off-the-shelf item becomes a kind of found object. In other cases, found objects themselves can be repurposed out of necessity, like the satellite dish that became a roof and inspired the design of a rocket ship at Verd-Mont Trailer Park. **Fig. 15** For Steve's project at the Wellspring Family Services playhouse, the Salt Lake City company 3Form donated a truckload of scrap eco-resin panels left over from high-end restaurant construction. Colors, sizes, and thicknesses varied but students solved the problem with two standard sizes (12"x 12" and 12" x 6") that they could mix and match to cover the playhouse's 3-by-7-foot panels with quilt-like patterns. **Figs. 16–17**

Materials for design/build can also come from the waste products of other building-related processes. In Cambodia Jim's students discovered that ash from the local process of burning rice husks in brick production can reduce the amount of cement in their concrete mixes. [see the Rural Kitchen project in the "Cases" chapter] For Steve's Supershed project at the University of Washington, twigs and vegetative material from the farm site filled the shed's wall cavity. Known as off-cuts, the leftover scraps from lumber milling offer raw material, though it is often short and sometimes dimensionally inconsistent. In one of my projects with students, a local lumber mill offered us two pallets of cypress and heart pine off-cuts. Though none were longer than two feet, this material constraint guided students in their design of a screen wall for a composting toilet facility and changing room.

Material properties play a part in the education. Wood is forgiving, and its familiarity offers a good entry point for all skill levels. Working with wood yields opportunities to maximize student involvement—hammers are readily available and nails are cheap, and using wood screws allows for mistakes and adjustments. As Steve readily points out, "Screwdrivers have a reverse," and impact drivers will not strip out the heads of screws. Chop saws and table saws allow all students the capability to do precise work, whether in the shop or on the site.

Steel requires time for welding instruction, and many schools' shops are not set up for steel fabrication. For the Mobile Perma-Kitchen design/build project at the University of Miami, every student learned to weld. In Mexico bricks and concrete were the primary materials for the University of Washington's projects. Jim notes that these building components were less precise than other systems but still allowed for design improvisation, particularly in the library's roof. **Fig. 18** Alternative materials and building systems lend themselves to mock-ups and trials—hay bales, bottles, tires, resin panels, and phone books. In John's 2006 studio at Yestermorrow, students designed and built an office kiosk for the Wilson Recycling Depot so that its walls could be lined with stacks of newspapers for insulation. The wall framing received and stored the bundled material as it awaited recycling. Such material finishing, similar to tiling, staining, sealing, and painting, offers repeatable tasks capable of engaging all skill levels.

Fig. 18 Students work on the roof of the Biblioteca Publica in Jiutepec, Mexico, 2001. The 20-foot span of the precast beams provided a constraint, but one that could be adapted to new forms, such as the curved roof.

CNC

Digital fabrication tools complement the design/build process. The CNC (computer numeric control) router offers accuracy and repetition, and can play very particular roles in full-scale production. The accuracy of the CNC's milling is both positive and negative. Students are building to a 1/16" tolerance at best, while the CNC can provide 1/1000". It is important not to let the machine (particularly in multiaxis milling) complicate the design/build project's necessary simplicity. The machine's capacity for repetition can assist the speed and efficiency of producing specific components. For the Guara Ki project, students milled marine plywood for the gusset plates, which made up the core of each framing bent. The curve of the plates would have been difficult to cut with a band saw or hand tools and even more challenging to replicate accurately. Jim planned the milled pieces to serve as references for lining up the columns and rafters that connect in each bent: "It made the project easy to put together, because it gave us the guideline to make everything line up." **Figs. 19–20**

The CNC is a tool among other tools. In design/build, it can do some things really well and relies on other tools for finishing. It is a part of an overall fabrication process. For the Coffee Kiosk, students used the CNC to cut hundreds of slots in the jambs, which are used to hold the louvers. While it would have been nearly impossible to produce these quantities by hand, making numerous cuts of 3/4" width and 3/8" depth out of the 1" x 6" rough-sawn cedar was no problem for the machine. But mock-ups indicated

The CNC is capable of doing incredibly accurate work and making tons of sawdust and noise, but you know how nice a pencil feels. [Steve]

the tear-out where the CNC bit emerges from the edge of the board at the slot's end. Students discovered that, after the CNC's work, they could rip the torn edges on a table saw, cleaning up the edge and achieving the proper width of the jamb.

There are also two sides to the CNC's efficiency. It is an excellent tool for reducing waste—components can be laid out to maximize a sheet of plywood's material. But despite this effectiveness and capacity for repetition, using the machine can increase logistics and setup. Depending on students' background and the shop setup, time must be allowed for students to learn the program that runs the machine as well as how to work safely with the tool. The process begins by importing drawing files from a computer-aided design (CAD) program like AutoCAD into a computer-aided manufacturing (CAM) program, which then converts the drawing into the code that controls the milling machine. During the conversion, the operator chooses particular tools, drill-bit size, and cutting speed and depth. **Fig. 21**

Fig. 20 Installation of milled pieces to connect columns and rafters in the Guara Ki project.

Fig. 19 University of Miami School of Architecture's CNC cutting gusset plates for the Guara Ki Bathhouse project, 2013.

Fig. 21 Students used UW's plasma cutter to fabricate metal components and to cut metal shear wall panels for the Children's Garden Cookery, 2014. Steve notes: "These functional panels take the shear in that outer row of trellis columns. Students worked on designs and presented them, and the class decided on the final design. A volunteer student team took responsibility for fabrication."

FEEDBACK

Slash. Design *slash* build. Design/build. Until recently, I used a hyphen rather than a slash to link *design* and *build*. But the hyphen is a tenuous bandage to the slash's insistent bend: the slash pushes them closer together. The slash is architectural: It makes a joint. It binds while it also slices. Set like a block plane's blade, it peels away distinctions of design and build. With sharpened precision, it allows the process, again in John's words, "to skate" through any "rough spots" between designing and building. Its angular profile is an emblem for a dynamic process. I was at first reluctant to ask the members of Jersey Devil if their use of the slash rather than hyphen was intentional—I thought they might tease about my overanalysis as an academic gloss on diacritics. But the slash in their group's name and in the programs they teach is by design. It also builds a word. [see "Day One" in the Process chapter]

> **It is import-ant to make a direct connection from the mind to the hand, to the tool, to the mate-rial. Only then is the true impli-cation of design revealed.** [Jim]

The slash between *design* and *build* indicates a unified process, one that singular terms cannot quite capture. John notes that *creating* comes close, and he recalls conversations with Yestermorrow's founder John Connell that suggest the closest English term is *making*—but *making* might place too much of an emphasis on fabrication, reducing the potential for design to continue to influence build. This term then becomes a tool, and *design/build* defines a working method to understand the connections between conceptual moti-vations and real-world conditions, between the intentions of design and the constraints of build.

The slash signals feedback. For Jim, the process is "constantly looping back on itself." When it is closely linked to build, design works alongside construction and sometimes even follows it, and this is how the process plays out—design, build, redesign.

Feedback links tool with process, and improvisation is made easier when the maker is also the designer. For Steve, it is "like an artist getting feedback from a sculpture as it evolves." **Figs. 22–23** This exchange is immediate for the craftsperson—John says it is "almost instantaneous," and he suggests that the designer must be more conscious of how feedback of materials and spaces might work. Jim summarizes: "There's a whole different connection to the project as a designer and as a builder. But if you become the same thing, it is a process. It's a process with constant feedback." John suggests that we "ride this process mindfully."

Feedback, in a more literal sense, also comes from the surrounding con-text and community where a project is built. As demonstrated by Jersey Devil, which typically closed out projects with a finishing party for the clients and construction teams, ribbon-cutting ceremonies and neighborhood picnics at a design/build project's completion begin a process of post-occupancy dialogue. More practically, following up on repairs or maintaining previous design/build projects continues the input-output interchange between studio and community. John notes: "Part of design/build education is maintaining buildings. If you think about it, some of the first jobs we ever had were exactly at the level of maintenance…adding blocking and framing where previous work had missed it. That's a form of feedback." And three decades of work in a particular place, as is the case with Steve in Seattle, make for a lot of callbacks and related feedback.

Feedback occurs between builder and building. Steve talks about how the building communicates to those who are making it. One circuit of this dialogue is at a one-to-one scale—building at full scale elicits responses on many levels. **Figs. 24–25** Jim has noticed there is a moment when the cameras

Fig. 22 Fremont Troll under construction, 1990.

Fig. 23 Fremont Troll under construction, 1990.

Fig. 24 With the Guara Ki project, the connection between skid foundation, joists, and wall supports was resolved with 2x2 boards as the other systems came together on the site. These connectors followed the methodology of bypass systems that allow for largely simple joints.

Fig. 25 Detail of connection in Guara Ki project.

come out. At the first hint of full-scale construction—a braced column, a partially framed deck, formwork readied for a concrete pour—there is a photo op. Mock-ups also capture this moment, when the one-to-one relation between design and construction becomes evident. With design *slash* build, design leans forward into construction's realm while build looks back to design, which, for those engaged in this process, continues until the last step.

JOHN RINGEL: In my understanding of 'design-slash-build,' we're looking to describe one process. We are looking for a word that describes something that in English has no real word. To talk about design and build or design-dash-build is to talk about approximations, but we're looking for the process that is design *build*. There's no separation. And I'm told that in the history of Yestermorrow Design/Build School, there have been serious debates about whether it's design-slash-build or design-dash-build, and the winning argument I've heard is that the process is something perhaps closest to the English word *making*. We're talking about making things, which is the intellect engaged with the hands, creating a feedback loop. So we're mushing together those two parts that we all know are a unified process; we're trying to make them into one.

JIM ADAMSON: We do the slash at University of Miami. John's right: it really does integrate the two closer together. When you use a hyphen, it creates a separation—two different processes—but it really isn't. Instead, it's a single process that is constantly looping back on itself.

STEVE BADANES: I think my students would rather have it be *build/design*.

CHARLIE HAILEY: That's similar to the idea of designing backward, which we touched on last time.

SB: Yes, design-build-redesign. And improvise. There's a whole lot more improvisation that goes on when the maker is also the designer.

JR: The conceptual advantage of the design/build model—a truly "hands-on approach"—over the model in which the designer hands off drawings to the builder is that both the process of documenting and the process of deciphering are streamlined. As architects, we make a perfect set of drawings and then hand them off to someone who inevitably starts scratching his or her head about what we really meant in the drawings. If we are the designer and builder, we skate through that rough spot.

MOCK-UP

Mock-ups are tests that help make the transition from design to construction. These full-scale assemblies investigate joints, walls, fastener patterns, even material effects like glazing's reflectivity. They serve both instructional and experimental purposes. They are precise and evanescent, contrived as well as improvised. For Jim, mock-ups are logical consequences of the design process:

Fig. 26 With the Motes Orchid Pavilion, students studied how wood slats might support privacy and maximize ventilation. Deliberation occurred after the frame had been constructed, and students mocked up systems of skip sheathing to determine optimum spacing.

Fig. 27 Slats as framework for orchids.

"When students struggle to express themselves verbally or in drawings, we give them the chance to mock something up full-scale. One student has an idea. Another sees it a different way, but they can't decide. Mock it up. And then it becomes obvious what the solution needs to be." **Figs. 26–27**

With the Coffee Kiosk, students used mock-ups as a study tool to explore louvers as a full-scale system, check the CNC mill's workability, and get a sense of both natural light's infiltration and artificial light's nighttime, lantern-effect glow.

Making a full-scale model tests ideas, materials, and details, and seeing a project in three dimensions further generates ideas. Mock-ups are equally didactic and experimental—they teach as well as speculate. They answer some questions while simultaneously probing previously unconsidered conditions, which can potentially raise other lines of inquiry. As John notes, "OK, now we know how to fabricate it, but what have we learned?" **Figs. 28–30**

Fig. 28 Students mocked up a section of the lamella roof in the third week of Steve's 2005 design/build project for the Arboretum Sunhouse.

Fig. 29 Concerns about wood degradation from weather exposure led students to cover the framing with multiwall polycarbonate sheets (a product sold as Polygal) for moisture and UV protection and for thermal insulation.

Fig. 30 Discussion (with University of Washington professor Ed Lebert) about full-scale mock-up and scale model of Arboretum Sunhouse.

Fig. 31 Scale model (1" = 1'-0")
for Motes Orchid Pavilion, 2009.

Fig. 32 Completed orchid
pavilion.

Mock-ups are also dummies. Early applications of this technique quite literally mocked what they were imitating. And in the design process, mock-ups—with their three-dimensional, now physical, form—do sometimes reveal the limitations of their drawn antecedents. Mock-ups can recalibrate drawings' dimensions, reveal material conflicts, show disconnections of joints, and expose flaws in fastening schedules. They can help us critique previous phases of the design process while providing a model and template for what we will do next.

Though not always considered a part of the mock-up family, sketch models are invaluable tools for moving the design process into the realm of the built. Like maquettes used by sculptors as scaled-down versions of their artwork, physical scale models are working drafts, rough but precise. They do not merely document results of the design process; they also prepare students to construct the project—a process of designing with the intention to build. **Figs. 31–32** With carefully constructed basswood models, a student's desk becomes a builder's yard of materials—miniature versions of stick lumber, joists, beams, rafters, studs, and purlins. **Fig. 33**

Fig. 33 Model-making during charette to design a prefabricated modular system for the Beacon Food Forest project, 2013.

This inventory developed from model making provides an accurate reference for material take-offs and estimates. The models can also demonstrate how the building responds to applied forces: pushing a finger against a 1-inch scale model reveals the racking of an unbraced frame, the stiffening of moment connections, the resistance added by bracing, or the lateral strength of a shear wall's sheathing. Model assembly is a dry run for full-scale construction—if students can build an accurate model, then they can build larger components. Models also help clients "see" the project and can serve as focal points for studio discussions. **Fig. 34**

Fig. 34 Helping Link project, 2010. Models convey ideas to clients in a physical form, often more familiar than the abstractions of drawings. In presentations, an audience will often crowd around the model as a theater in the round.

And then mock-ups bring parts of the sketch model to full scale. Although jumping scale may be daunting for students and young professionals (even if they are familiar with model making), mock-ups adapt what architecture students already do really well. As Steve points out, architecture students are well prepared to "understand the flexibility of designing in three dimensions with the real object." In mock-ups, tectonic components themselves now take up actual space: joints become architecture, and framing members—like joists that were previously understood nominally by their two-by-six dimensions—now concede to actual measurements in which the two is in fact one and a half inches and the six is five and a half inches.

Drawings, like mock-ups, can in some cases help prepare for the jump in scale. Design/build instructors' approach to construction drawings varies, unless they are necessary for permitting. **Figs. 35–36** Some favor treating detailed drawings as a transition between the design and build components of the process or as means of documenting what has been built—the "as-built" drawing set. But Jim maintains an idea that these drawings are "as-being-builts." With this perspective, they still serve as transitions between designing and building—but in a more fluid process that allows building also to transform drawings. In some cases, full-scale drawings aid such translations by clarifying dimensions and allowing construction details to come to life as a one-to-one kit of parts.

Mock-ups provide feedback. They tell us things that we may not have previously seen or understood. In mock-ups, Steve uncovers the "variety and vagaries of materials that aren't evident in the drawings." These full-scale studies lend themselves to multiples and generate an iterative process of discovery. As a set of explorations, mock-ups speak to each other—and to us—about materiality, connections, strength, aesthetics, and local resources.

Mock-ups are an important part of the editing process and often serve as three-dimensional Ockham's razors, hewing toward the simplest solutions. **Figs. 37–38** Jim has also pointed out that mock-ups facilitate group decision making: at full scale, everyone can more easily see what the issues are. For the 2013 Guara Ki bathroom facility, Jim's students mocked up sheathing and louvered systems. In the former, students studied differences between vertical and horizontal orientations. In the latter, they sought to understand the sight lines that were critical for privacy as well as ventilation. **Figs. 39–40**

Framing Plan

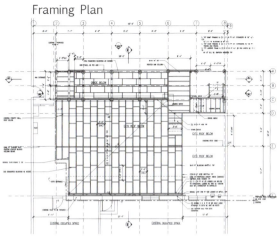

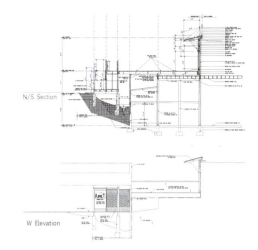

N/S Section

W Elevation

Fig. 35 Plan drawing of Helping Link project, 2010. For this project, code officials requested a detailed set of construction drawings, which satisfied building department requirements but also linked the studio's mock-ups and scale models.

Fig. 36 North-south section and west elevation drawings of Helping Link project.

Fig. 38 The complete truss system was later assembled and tested, leading up to work with the project's new client, the Lao Highlands Association.

Fig. 40 The outcome of the mock-up was a chevron profile that ventilates, offers privacy, and resists warping with its glued and brad-nailed diagonal connection.

Fig. 37 In Steve's 2008 project for the Lao Highland community pavilion, students tested the strength of the middle truss of the teaching pavilion's roof.

Fig. 39 Students tested components and profiles for the 2013 Guara Ki Bathhouse project.

Mock-ups are tools of visualization. Building a test case at full scale makes it possible to see problems, pitfalls, and possibilities. This way of seeing also prepares students for professional practice, in which many firms first assemble full-scale building sections, particularly in collaboration with engineers, to test proposed systems and components. Such mock-ups also facilitate communication with clients who might then better understand a project's building systems, scale, and material palette. Even though mock-ups cost time, they often save money and help avoid misunderstandings as well as miscalculations.

Mock-ups provide context. They offer a setting for decisions about details, and Jim makes sure this visualization is a part of his design/build studios: "Students really want to design it right down to the last detail but they don't really have the context until they build it. Once construction starts, even if it's only partially built, some decisions are easy. They might spend days debating in the design phase, but they don't really have enough physical feedback at that stage to make informed decisions."

Like mock-ups, jigs are full-scale templates for what will be made. They bring mock-ups full circle by returning to the drawing board, sending the studio into the workshop, and linking shop to construction site. Once they are set up, they allow repetitive and precise production of components, whether by cutting, fitting, or fastening.

When Jim and Steve set up a jig for braced frame bents at Yestermorrow, they introduce the process as a form of drawing in which one inch equals one inch. **Fig. 41** Edges, center lines, overlapping pieces, cut lines, and fastener locations are inscribed on plywood surfaces raised on a work bench. Blocks and drill holes further register the assembly process and make the jig a reference tool for construction. **Fig. 42** This mock-up becomes a dance floor—one reason we call it a "jig"—that choreographs students' movement as they assemble each frame. **Fig. 43**

 **The bypass system lends itself well to jig construction. You can make structural bents so that walls and roof are an integrated package, a 'bypass package.'** [Jim]

Fig. 41 Jig for Shelburne Farms composting toilet structure, Yestermorrow, 2013.

Fig. 42 Drill hole jigs for Wellspring Family Services playhouse project, 2009.

Fig. 43 Jig for Guara Ki Bathhouse, 2013.

FIT

Fit seeks harmony as it negotiates design concepts with ways of building, works between problem and solution, and physically coordinates the joining of materials. Make it fit. This is Robert Geddes's call for a Hippocratic oath of architecture and echoes design/build's general precepts as well as the particular ethos of Jersey Devil, whose members were students during Geddes's tenure as dean of Princeton's School of Architecture. With design/build, a project's problems as defined by site, client, and program immediately come into contact with proposed solutions and the realities of construction, and the process of defining problems directly meets the process of resolving them. Fit measures the adaptations that result. It is a tool that mediates suitability, not absolutely but by degrees. By making it fit, build redefines the problem that design first encountered.

“ **There is always the observation: 'I cut it twice, and it's still too short.'''** [John]

Instructors can, to a degree, plan for fit. As Steve notes, design/build studios that are integrated within a school's curriculum must provide learning outcomes appropriate to the coursework's overall pedagogical goals. And small projects are best—scope of work must suit short time periods and limited budgets. Even the most modest projects give rise to complexities and challenges, but can contribute to the richness of an architect's education. Pavilions, decks, sheds, and kiosks make for appropriate scales that can be completed in eleven weeks (University of Washington's quarter system) or sixteen weeks (University of Miami's semester), and even in two weeks when work continues all day, as it does in Yestermorrow's Public Interest Design/Build, or the nine afternoons of construction in John's Home Design/Build class. **Fig. 44**

Fit also guides how you build. In framed construction, modified bypass systems are often developed to match students' emergent skill levels. With beams and joists that effortlessly slip past columns, it is easier to conceal a bad cut, there are fewer tight miter or butt joints, and metal clips and joist hangers are avoided. Instead, bolted connections tie together the temporarily clamped assemblies. A tool of visual aesthetics and pedagogy alike, the bypass system also makes legible a project's hierarchy of materials. **Fig. 45** For Steve's projects at Danny Woo Community Garden in Seattle, the bypass system resonated with indigenous architecture from the gardeners' home countries of Japan, China, and Korea, where the traditional wood framing of temples often forms bracketed and extended corners. **Fig. 46**

Fig. 44 The concession stand and ticket booths for the University of Wisconsin–Milwaukee's women's soccer field was a semester-long project, 2001. Top: Jim, John, and Steve at the dedication; bottom: concession stand.

Fit informs where you build and what you build. Being on site allows students to check orientation as well as fine-tune layouts and, ultimately, understand how a project fits—or conflicts—with its context. When his Home Design/Build studio works on site-built projects, John brings an easel with paper to the site to help visualize the studio's ideas. **Fig. 47** Sketches, site plans, and diagrams provide a direct link between conversations about the design scheme and the site's context. Steve describes this editing process as the drive toward a "legible, simple idea." Whereas design studios might

Fig. 45 In the 2003 Danny Woo Community Garden project, framed construction used the bypass method to facilitate construction and to reflect the gardeners' native architecture.

Fig. 46 Danny Woo Community Garden gathering place, with structures using bypass construction.

Fig. 47 Chicken coop project, Yestermorrow, 2012. For site-specific projects, John's Home Design/Build studio often uses an easel for early schematic and site design sketches.

Fig. 48 For the coffee kiosk project, Jim and Rocco used a prefabricated aluminum frame as a base for the framing. This reference—a simple square measuring 7 feet on a side—provided a foundation for fit.

Fig. 49 Overall frame of Coffee Kiosk.

explore multiple solutions, design/build studios must choose the one that fits. Keep it simple. **Figs. 48–49**

Fit also involves tolerance—both in the way that materials go together and in the way people work together. Everybody belongs and contributes, and, like people, joints must agree on degrees of inaccuracy. Two materials or systems that meet must each sustain some amount of difference. To quantify this, John uses 1/32" as the goal—though rarely attained—of his design/build studio. Steve and Jim look for 1/16". Even this number is an ideal, and I remember calling out a "heavy sixteenth" to Jim, who laughed and said, "You mean more like a three thirty-second." These figures are the allowable amount of play, error, or "slop" between assembled components. As they seek consensus and work collaboratively, design/build students must also tolerate each other and find play in their differences. And, as Jim notes, instructors must expect and accept student mistakes, just as clients must be patient with deadlines. Fit is a tool that prepares students to build *and* design, because it speaks to relations of people and place.

CONSENSUS

Collaboration plays a critical role for practicing and teaching design/build. When Jim says, "and you're inviting all your friends to come join you," he captures this spirit and alludes to the joys of a multidisciplinary process. In Jersey Devil's work, these "friends" refer to everyone involved in each project, including local fabricators, woodworkers, artists, sculptors, painters, mosaic tilers, contractors, architects, and land excavators. **Figs. 51–53** Their working method shows how jobsites become open-air studios, labs for experimentation, and learning-by-doing classrooms. Their penchant for working together—a three-way collaboration that extends to a broader group—translates well to what they now ask students to do. It also, in turn, lends itself to the increasingly collaborative nature of professional work, particularly when design and build overlap. Design/build needs collaboration, which works best with consensus.

Consensus is a tool. In the design/build studio, it is essential that students agree on a design scheme. Unanimity helps keep everyone fully engaged throughout the entire process. Steve and Jim have developed techniques and approaches for establishing a collaborative atmosphere—what is sometimes called group "buy-in." They seek consensus at the outset of studios and projects. Steve plays devil's advocate by suggesting that perhaps he should design the project himself. Despite the competitive atmosphere in studio that often promotes the best individual designs, it is a community of students. As John points out, competition is not the answer if the "class wants the best collaborative design." Steve says it becomes clear that there has to be a way to "come up with an idea that everybody is on board with." Otherwise, the construction phase and class dynamics will be painful.

In the first or second class, Steve and Jim divide the studio into two groups, usually counting off around the room. They ask each group to list the positive and negative aspects of working in groups—"all the really fabulous things" as well as the "really bad things" about working collaboratively. After ten to fifteen minutes of brainstorming, the whole studio reconvenes, and the instructor asks for responses, alternating between groups. The discussion generates a list of pros and cons—usually about twelve of each—on either side of a large sheet of butcher paper. Steve and Jim then divide the students into two different groups and ask them to "make a list of how to reinforce the good stuff and mitigate the bad stuff." The groups come back together for a second time, and the instructor fills the central column with each group's responses. [see sidebar]

The entire activity takes little more than an hour, but the lists will remain in the studio as exemplars of this initial process—reminders and models throughout the project. This process not only serves as an exercise for talking about

Fig. 51 Jersey Devil construction crew for the Hoagie House, McLean, Virginia, 1983.

Fig. 52 Finishing party for Room for a Forest project, 2013.

Fig. 53 Jersey Devil finishing party for the Palmetto House, Redland, Florida, 1987.

group work but also models consensus building itself, and a similar method will facilitate the design charrette that follows. Steve developed this exercise as an introduction to collaborative methods and offers it as an alternative to competition-based design work. [see "Group" in the Process chapter]

"In architectural education, they've been taught that creativity is a solitary endeavor and that if you just go home and stay up all night and come back with the perfect scheme, you're a hero. That's not going to work in a group. And if you pick somebody's idea—a lot of schools do this with competition—then you get one person or small group who's on the spot and a bunch of other people who are reluctant to participate because they feel their ideas were better, and this creates a hierarchy." [Steve]

Building consensus among participants parallels the building process. Steve notes, "It's not a silver bullet, but it fleshes out all that's going to go wrong," and it makes way for what can go right. Establishing the tool of consensus comes first, then agreeing on an idea and design scheme, followed by negotiating the realities of construction. Collective opinion prepares the group for the inevitable realization that the design will change—"When we start to build it, it becomes obvious that we screwed up or that there's a better way." Steve cautions against following one person's scheme, because "a competition creates a poisonous hierarchy that doesn't work." In the classroom setting, consensus helps keep egos in check.

Maintaining consensus requires communication, a continual vetting of ideas. Meetings at the beginning and end of work sessions allow for planning, scrutinizing particular solutions, and addressing individual concerns within the group context. With consensus as a process, there is constant dialogue: "There's a lot of communication going on so that when the building communicates something to us, there's a chance we might be able to do something better or do something differently. We can resolve that fairly quickly and keep

To have group ownership of the project is in many ways more important than having the most amazing project that could have been designed by one person. [Steve]

GENERATING CONSENSUS AND WORKING IN GROUPS

(derived from a studio Steve led in 2004; Jim uses similar techniques to illustrate the pros, cons, and possible solutions of group work)

Pros (+)

Many skills
Diversity of ideas
Production
Leadership
  opportunities
More resources
Learning from each
  other
Division of labor
Interdependence
Carpool lane
Fun
Share expense
Physical diversity

Cons (-)

Schedule conflicts
Reaching consensus
Keeping everyone busy
Personality conflicts
Bad communication
Accountability
Compromise and LCD
  (lowest common
  denominator)
Leadership issue
Distractions
Organization issues
Love triangles
(Inter)dependence
Slackers
Punctuality

Solutions

Self-motivation
Mission statement
Group memory
Respect
Proactive participation
Communication (phone,
  email)

Inventory of skills
Humility
Name tags
Humor
Patience
Beer
Set deadlines

moving." At Yestermorrow, Jim and Steve often call students together and use the partially built project as a chalkboard, clamping and tacking up possible solutions for the group's assessment. Consensus is a tool for continuing forward—"to keep everybody going ahead."

With a wry smile, Steve remarks on how much students love the consensus exercise, which offers them a chance to grumble about "all the people who slack off and who dominate groups." But they also begin to realize that groups generate "more ideas, more productivity, and more fun." Group work allows for a collective irreverence that has the mock seriousness of a party, a building party, a camping trip, an event that you've invited your friends to, a place built on the social as much as the technical, and a place of learning by doing for students, instructors, and professionals alike.

FUN

The work of manual labor can be fun—*homo faber* can become *homo ludens*. Play extends fun into the realm of work, and the freedom it offers carves a temporary sphere of activity from daily life. But rules, duration, and locale also factor into the ludic. With design/build, making things combines work and play and parallels the mix of intuition with technical skill found in improvisation—what John sees as the mix of inspiration and exertion. Knowing *how* to do informs what you *can* do.

Construction sites are adventure playgrounds. **Fig. 54** Like children and alchemists, Jersey Devil's members experiment with methods of construction, space, and materials on the jobsite. As pranksters, they subvert rules without quite breaking them. As educators, they summon both practiced idealism and puckish irreverence. Learning is elevated with fully engaged senses amid the workaday context of the construction site. It's like going to camp, as one of Jim's students noted. Or running away and joining the circus, as Steve recalls former editor of *Progressive Architecture* Mark Alden Branch's appraisal of Jersey Devil. **Figs. 55–56**

The fun of design/build is in the collaborative process—its interactions, the project's formal associations, and the act of making itself. According to legend, the group's eponymous demon brought spirited mischief to its New Jersey surroundings. That Pine Barrens house—their first building after architecture school—looked like a snail. Locals felt sure the Jersey Devil was again playing tricks, and the name stuck. Later the Natchez Beach Pavilion in Seaside evoked sea monsters and sailboats. **Fig. 57** And in Seattle you can walk all over the Fremont Troll, like a great piece of play equipment. **Fig. 58**

With Steve's playscape project for Seattle's Experimental Education Unit (EEU), which focuses on cognitive development in early childhood, Jersey Devil's work came full circle. In 1972 he and John built the Arthurpod, a bug-like climbing structure. **Fig. 59** Twenty-four years later, the Neighborhood Design/Build Studio worked with the EEU, and children clambered up and down play equipment suspended from the facility's ceiling. **Fig. 60** Activities of design/build informed activities of play. Cut, join, and fold made it possible to crawl, bounce, and roll. And in the process, architecture students had fun building as well as playing with—and like—children. In another playground project, which had fun with a found object at Yestermorrow, a satellite dish inspired ideas of play, fantasy, and spaceships when it became the core element of Verd-Mont Trailer Park's play structure.

Harnessing the joy of construction, design/build's immediacy can change the way we perceive things. Discarded materials become roofs, walls, floors; and architecture can be trolls, bugs, rockets, and dragons. To build the play structure for Warren Elementary School, John's design/build students squeezed into tiny spaces and clambered through tiny doors, mimicking the movements of the kids who would play there. **Fig. 61** John often speaks about

Fig. 54 Like at an adventure playground, children help move bricks on the Rural Kitchen construction site in Siem Reap, Cambodia, MIT School of Architecture and Planning, 2010.

Fig. 55 Football House, Woodside, California, 1976.

Fig. 56 The Stairway to Nowhere, 1988. Steve recalls that Ken Frampton called the project a belvedere, noting that it was a good place to hang out.

Fig. 57 Natchez Beach Pavilion, Seaside, Florida, 1992.

Fig. 58 Fremont Troll, dedication ceremony, 1990.

Fig. 59 Arthurpod play structure, George and Lois De Menil house, Princeton, New Jersey, 1972.

Fig. 60 Suspended Climber Playground Structures, University of Washington Health Science Experimental Education Unit, 1995.

the "pleasure" and "delight" of architecture, and it is this liberating joy of using tools, reanimating cast-off materials, and building for others that characterizes design/build. **Fig. 62**

CH: How do pleasure and delight play a part in design/build education?

JR: It ought to be fun. It's work but it should be fun.

SB: A goal most people have in their life is to have some fun, and if you take it even further, it includes enjoying your work. That's why design/build in the studio generates a lot of interest. We're laughing all the time, they love to build, and working in groups is potentially a lot more fun than struggling on your own. One of the students said to me today, "This is like going to camp."

JA: "And I'm getting credits for it."

SB: Is it not supposed to be fun? Also, there's a sort of irreverence and idealism that is part of the collaborative process that I think the students find appealing, and it's fun.

CH: And you convey that sense of fun to your students now.

SB: They see that these are guys who have a lot of laugh lines and have had pretty good lives. I mean, you can't wipe that smile off Jim's face.

JR: But that might mean we need to hire surrogates pretty soon.

Fig. 61 John's 1992 Home Design/Build studio project at Yestermorrow for the Warren Elementary play structure.

Fig. 62 Testing the weight of a floor panel for the Everglades Eco-Tent project, University of Miami Design/Build, 2012.

TRICKS

Tricks of the building trade are not tools of deception but are instead didactic reminders and useful expedients. In design/build, this latter category helps translate studio's design production and drawing techniques to the construction site and forms what Steve has called "the huge Mayline in the sky"—that is, the idea of drafting and making at full scale. Strategies for paralleling, squaring, and leveling ease this transition, and revitalize and reinitiate the design process as students see the implications—now writ large—of what they have drawn in studio. The verbal equivalents of these tricks are the aphorisms that resonate across the jobsite.

PARALLEL

Make it parallel first, then check for plumb. Imagine framing a wall with wood studs. Initially, the frame will rest horizontally on a platform or concrete pad. First, cut the top and bottom plates. Then, cut the studs. In both cases, as John says, cut them the same length. The plates run the wall's length, and the studs measure the wall's height, minus the depth of the two plates. On the horizontal surface, position the two plates side by side and run the measuring tape down their length, marking each stud's location on both plates. This mark, consistent between the two plates, ensures the studs will be parallel. Separate the two plates and locate the perpendicular studs between them so that each end hits its mark. Fasten stud ends to the plates. Even if the frame is skewed—what Steve calls "wackity"—it will still be parallel. Now, the frame can be raised vertically and plumbed along each axis. **Figs. 63–64**

Figs. 63–64 Setting up the skids for the Guara Ki Bathhouse, 2013. Similar to framing a stud wall, cross pieces between the two beams are cut the same length and their locations are marked along each side.

SQUARE

You can also square the frame. Recall high school geometry and the 3-4-5 triangle. This process translates Jim's drafting triangle and Steve's giant Mayline to the jobsite's scale—imagine a plastic triangle the size of a smart car. Measure six feet along one edge and eight feet along another, connecting the two end points on a diagonal. This diagonal forms the hypotenuse and needs to measure ten feet to draw together the squared right angle where the two shorter sides meet. Use a steel measuring tape rather than rope or string, because fibers stretch. **Fig. 65** Jim introduces geometry's logic on the first day of studio with a handout that ties circular form to rectilinear layouts. [see sidebar] By the same geometric rules, you can also check for square by comparing diagonal measurements across a rectangular frame, whether it is a wall, a floor, or a roof system. Pull a measuring tape from one corner to the opposite corner and repeat for the other diagonal pairing. **Fig. 66** If they match, the ›

Fig. 65 Laying out footings for the Coffee Kiosk (2014) and measuring sides to determine perpendicular corners.

Fig. 66 Measuring diagonals to check for square.

SQUARING: 3-4-5 TRIANGLE

Jim introduces geometry's logic and math on the first day of studio with a handout that ties circular form to rectilinear layouts.

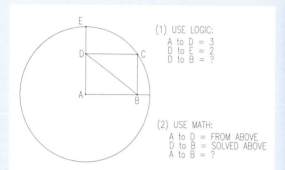

(1) USE LOGIC:
A to D = 3
D to E = 2
D to B = ?

(2) USE MATH:
A to D = FROM ABOVE
D to B = SOLVED ABOVE
A to B = ?

Figs. 68–69 Steve used geometries similar to Jim's logic and math exercise to fabricate the laminated beams for Bradner Gardens Park's central pavilion, shown in Gould Hall's court and installed at the site, 2000.

corners are square. If they don't, the parallelogram can be adjusted with bar clamps, framed braces, or sledgehammer taps. Recheck for square.

LEVEL

In the late 1980s Jersey Devil made T-shirts that depicted the Hoagie House's dramatic cantilever over a grinning sprite riding a box-beam level, captioned "on the level." **Fig. 70** The leveling process shadows you around the site with joists, beams, decks, floors, sills, steps, and landings. And its tools are diverse, sometimes mysterious, but always essential and absolute.

Jim, John, and Steve teach how to use the builder's level, known historically as the "dumpy level" for its short and stout telescope attached to a spirit level. **Fig. 71** These "dumpier," optically leveled versions effectively teach precision and accuracy, although automatic and laser

Fig. 70 Original 1986 Hoagie House T-shirt with Jersey Devil "on the level."

Fig. 71 Steve works with a student using the builder's level to lay out the Arboretum's Sunhouse, 2005.

LEVELING: WATER TUBE LEVEL

The water-filled tube provides a simple and portable method of leveling on the construction site. The water surfaces at each end will maintain level. This technique requires two people and the following materials:

Minimum setup
→ Water source (water can be colored or muddy to increase visibility)
→ Transparent plastic tubing, 6–10 mm inside diameter
→ Length varies; in some applications, a minimum of forty feet is recommended, but shorter lengths have worked well for Steve and Jim at Yestermorrow

Optional setup
→ Including the above materials
→ two poles or staves, each 6 feet long
→ four straps for attaching tubes to vertical poles

Note: Allow time (typically five seconds) for water to "find" level. Air bubbles should be avoided—tap with finger to remove.

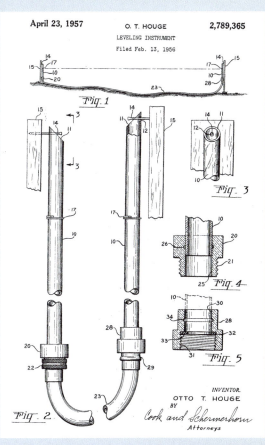

Figs. 72 Flexible tube water level setup used for establishing contour elevations. A much simpler, yet equally accurate, version can be made.

levels are now common in design/build studios. Four-foot-long box-beam and I-beam levels are standard tools to check for plumb and for level along shorter runs of material. Steve warns that the smaller torpedo levels are misleading; their best use is plumbing (the kind with pipes and fixtures) applications.

On coastal sites, visible horizon lines serve as natural reference tools for leveling. You can readily and accurately match the top of a beam to the crisp contour where water and sky meet. If your site is landlocked, water tube levels bring the waterline to you. As construction progresses, students can understand the site as a matrix of vertical and horizontal lines, the occupiable version of what they have previously only visualized in computer-aided drafting. On small projects, Jim says that he tends to use the water level as a "quick, cheap, accurate and easily understandable" method of leveling. He and Steve often use the technique in their summer studios at Yestermorrow.

STRING LINE

Use string line with gauge blocks to set posts and check alignments. **Fig. 73** The blocks provide offsets to keep the material, which is being measured and checked, from coming into contact with the string. String lines also set foundation locations. **Figs. 74–75**

STORY POLE

Once a benchmark (a point of reference for standardizing elevation heights) is established on the site, another tool—the story pole—serves the construction process but also strengthens these didactic connections. Relative to the benchmark, ticked marks on story (also "storey") poles record heights of platforms, plates, headers, landings, and work surfaces. Such tools help visualize datums—whether previously noted in sketches and diagrams or recorded as elevation marks in construction drawings.

Fig. 73 String line marks the end of the rafter tails for the Helping Link community center's roof extension. A standard block was used as a spacer to set the rafters against the string line.

Figs. 74–75 In week four of Steve's 2008 University of Washington studio project, students set string lines on batter boards to locate footings.

Fig. 76 John explains how to use the story pole (or "stadia rod") for the framing of the firewood storage shed project at Yestermorrow in 2011.

Carried around like a diviner's rod, they quite literally tell the story of construction and, by association, the design narratives. **Fig. 76**

ANGLES

Setting, transferring, and marking angles can be difficult. The angle bevel can be adjusted and set to scribe wood for cutting or to line up the chop saw. You can also use the speed square in its traditional method—pivoting at the apex and rotating the hypotenuse through its tick marks until the desired angle is found. Jim recommends that roof slopes be whole numbers. For example, a "3 in 12" specifies a 3-inch rise and a 12-inch run. Rafter layout tools like Swanson speed squares quickly determine angles for common, jack, and hip rafter cuts.

STRAIGHT LINES

If the board is straight, use the combination square with a pencil (it has a little notch in the middle of its short end) to scribe a line parallel to the edge. A chalk line is useful as a straight reference when the board is warped.

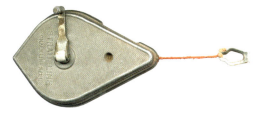

LEVER

John reminds students that they're smarter than 2x4s but not stronger. The trick is combining usefulness with ingenuity. He invokes the lever:

"It strikes me that a lot of what happens in my class is demonstrating the utility of things most people only have a glimmer of understanding of. The prime example is the lever, which is a way to magnify our strength through a basic principle that can be used in infinite number of ways if we are clever. On site, the first time we are trying to wrestle a warped or otherwise distorted framing member into place and brute force is not working, I will ask: 'Where is Archimedes? And where would he stand?' This leads to the quote 'Give me a place to stand and a lever long enough, and I will move the world'—most people know the reference, but have never had a need to apply it and see its power. After successfully applying some trick of leverage, a toe-nail, standing at the free end of the board and using its length to line it up where a second person is putting a nail, using a 2x as a lever, a clamp, or a jack, or a crowbar, I will then introduce the idea that leverage matches our intellect with a 2x4's strength."

> **Cut to the right or left of your line, because the line represents the edge of your piece and every saw blade has a thickness.** [Jim]

APHORISM

Like tricks of building, turns of phrase have always played an important part on the construction site. Aphorisms break monotony, recall rules of thumb, and prompt safety. I remember Jim quoting from *Modern Carpentry*, a textbook for students and experienced carpenters alike. Willis H. Wagner summarized his book, first published in 1969, as "an easy-to-understand cyclopedia of basic information on modern building methods and materials." In the text, side-bars deliver insights and reminders with the lead-in "Handy says..." **Fig. 77** On page ninety-six of my 1973 edition, Handy, a latter-day Bob the Builder grasping a curved-claw hammer and dressed smartly in a cap and apron, makes an early appearance in the footings and foundations section: "Check the formwork carefully before placing the concrete. A form that fails during the pouring will waste material and cause a lot of extra work."

HANDY SAYS:

"Maintain a high level of accuracy in laying out and in cutting floor framing members. The strength of the assembly depends on all the parts fitting tightly together."

Fig. 77 "Handy says..." from *Modern Carpentry*.

Like Handy's prompts, aphorisms have long served builders as mnemonics, rules, and rubrics. Such turns of phrase are also called "saws," and it is no surprise that "saw" as tool and "saw" as maxim share origins in the wisdom of storytelling and the cutting power of speech. Aphorisms speak to design/build's directness and its sometimes overtly simple approach, not unlike a master carpenter's economy of movement and material. "Measure twice, cut once" reminds us to conserve material and avoid systematic errors of measurement. It came in handy for Jim's University of Miami students during the Eco-Tent project in the Florida Everglades: the dimensions of the framing lumber differed from the drawings' dimensions, because the students had substituted heat-treated pine for the pressure-treated wood that was originally specified, the width-to-depth ratio was not square as originally drawn, and the actual dimensions of the platform meant that walls and plates needed to be longer than expected. **Fig. 78** These verifications and discoveries prevented later discrepancies that would have added unwanted inches to the overall construction.

Fig. 78 Testing the framing of the Everglades Eco-Tent project, University of Miami Design/Build, 2012.

APHORISMS

Jersey Devil aphorisms:
→ Measure twice, cut once.
→ Measure once, cut twice.
→ Do not mess with a hippie while he is stoned on work. [recalled by John, from Mr. Natural Comics]
→ Get the right tool for the job. [also from Mr. Natural Comics]
→ It will be there in the morning. [Leon Barth's way of saying it was time to quit for the day.]
→ Where's it going to go? [Leon's common response when asked whether something was sufficiently braced structurally]
→ Another design opportunity… [from John, as a response to a mistake or unanticipated event]
→ It's just as easy to do a good cut as a bad one. [from Jim]

→ Strive for perfection and you get good results, strive for just good results and you get mediocrity. [from Jim]
→ If you work with your hands, you are a laborer. If you work with your hands and mind, you are an artisan. If you work with your hands, mind, and soul, you are an artist. [observed by Jim on the wall of Yestermorrow's south studio]
→ Let's see what Handy says… [Steve's recollection of Jim referencing Modern Carpentry]
→ You're smarter than the 2x4.

Sayings I have heard elsewhere but never on Jersey Devil's jobsite:
→ The painter will fix it.
→ You're fired when you hit the ground.
→ Good enough for government work.
→ Can't see it from my house.
→ The sheetrockers will cover it.

SB: "Measure once, cut twice," I suppose it's so.

JA: "Measure once, cut twice." That's the opposite…

SB: Right, measure zero times and cut a whole bunch until it fits.

JR: There's always the observation: I cut it twice and it's still too short.

Jersey Devil's aphorisms demonstrate how the construction site inspires a way of living and teaching and how professional life makes room for continued education, tapping a mock-serious tone but tracking deeper into traditions of craft and its broader significance. At the end of *Walden*, Thoreau petitions "Give me a hammer, and let me feel for the furring" and turns this commonplace activity into moral code: "Every nail driven should be as another rivet in the machine of the universe, you carrying on the work."

PITFALLS

Pitfalls are an unavoidable part of the design/build process. Instructors must not only manage work schedules, group dynamics, and budgetary concerns, but also administrate danger, difficulty, and error. It is difficult to measure risk in design/build, and uncertainty on the jobsite is best controlled with safety measures and constant vigilance.

RISK

Risk management departments at universities have strategies for addressing potential liability associated with a design/build studio. In some cases, students sign a Hold Harmless Agreement, waiving claims, assuming degrees of risk, and releasing the institution's liabilities. In other cases, universities also require the design/build studio's clients to sign a contract that holds the institution harmless from any problems or claims. In a third administrative scenario, the University of Washington's risk managers issue Steve a certificate of insurance each year.

MISTAKES

Apart from safety concerns, mistakes can become tools for learning as well as design opportunities. Just as the bricoleur makes do with what is at hand, the designer/builder must sometimes integrate errors and improvise within an ongoing design process. Design/build's linkage of concept and construction also allows students to take risks—within safety's parameters—and experiment with sometimes unexpected results. This exchange is one of the many tools that make up the design/build process discussed in the next chapter.

Another pitfall not directly associated with safety is scope creep. Here, the risk is not in health or safety but in not completing the project on time and within budget. The size of the project is a critical element to calibrate with resources of budget and labor. [see "Scope Creep" in "Groundwork"]

LIABILITY

Many design/build programs ask students to sign a waiver or release form. Steve receives a certificate of liability insurance from the university each year. Most institutions have a risk management department that can help with liability and legal issues. In some cases, the university will require the design/build client to sign a contract holding the institution harmless for any problems. At Yestermorrow, students receive a handout about safety and fill out a form that asks participants about allergies and whom to contact in case of emergencies. But in all cases, as Steve notes, "The best way to avoid problems—knock on wood—is to do a responsible job, supervise very closely, and don't create dangerous situations." John concurs: "The bottom line is you have to be vigilant."

SAFETY

When John says, "You have to be vigilant," he is speaking to instructors and students alike. Safety in design/build is both mindset and set of practices. It is, as Steve says, a "class within a class." With each part of the process, instructors move through the studio to assess students' abilities and safety practices, and to teach alternative methods of construction that avoid hazard and risk. Your responsibility as a design/build teacher is a lot more multifaceted than your responsibility as a boss on the jobsite; meanwhile, students have a responsibility not to overstate their abilities and to ask for help and instruction when needed. In his studios, John works with the initial assumption that no one knows how to use tools, which he introduces one by one as the project requires it. Even if students assert competence with a particular tool, "We tell them we believe them, but for safety reasons, all students will need to be evaluated by a teacher before they are able to use the tool unsupervised." And Jim and Rocco offer similar demonstrations of how to use, maintain, and store tools.

> **A tool is something that extends your capabilities. It's magic what it can do, but it can also bite you.** [Steve]

John provides a dual message: tools can be dangerous but you can readily control that danger with appropriate practices and techniques. Safety is not just about avoiding injury—it also helps link body and tool through confidence, control, and comfort. Used properly, tools feel good in your hand. They augment reach, power, and speed. You work with the tool, not against it. At the same time, you shouldn't be too comfortable, and mindfulness keeps you aware of limitations and ready for the unexpected. Jim summarizes safety as a cultivation of mindfulness and respect:

"That's part of teaching how to use tools. You have to respect the tool and know that it has the potential to injure you. There are ways to use this tool and it will be your best friend, and there are ways that it will really hurt. Have respect for the tool and be mindful of it. I think about it all the time when I'm using the table saw."

Steve attributes his and Jim's particular vigilance with the table saw to decades of site-built work with only circular saws. Despite years of experience, and actually as a result of those years of experience, Jersey Devil's focus on safety combines a virtuoso's skilled confidence with a learner's studied approach.

Safety extends beyond the operation of tools. It includes keeping site and shop in good order, wearing appropriate equipment and clothing, and practicing safe techniques such as clamping and bracing during construction. Safety also connects with the way a project is carried out. With the shorter schedule at Yestermorrow, instructors regularly work alongside students. With longer projects, students have more time to gain experience with tools, and they can carry out most of the construction.

Fig. 79 Jim shows his bandaged thumb from an injury sustained while teaching the Home Design/Build course at Yestermorrow in the 1990s.

SAFETY GUIDELINES

→ Always support and stabilize work.

→ Wear eye and ear protection.

→ Avoid distraction.

→ Always be aware of what is behind you.

→ Always wear proper gear and safety protection.

→ Always follow proper procedures for your own and others' safety.

→ Always use all tools only for their intended purpose after confirming they are in proper working order.

→ Always be aware of what is going on all around you.

→ Always keep the jobsite free of debris, cords, and other tripping hazards.

→ Always communicate with others around you before you start an operation that might affect them.

→ Do not be distracted by others or distract others while they are involved in an operation.

→ In the studio: Watch where your fingers are when using utility knives.

CLOTHING

→ Sturdy shoes (no open toes)

→ Work pants (canvas or denim)

→ Hat (soft for sun protection)

→ Hard hat

→ Safety glasses / sunglasses

→ Work gloves

→ Sunblock

→ Jewelry (rings, necklaces, earrings) is discouraged.

→ Hair should be tied up.

"Here at Yestermorrow, where time's a little tighter, the teachers do a lot of building. At the University of Washington, we try to have the students do just about everything. If there's a nasty overhead SkilSaw cut, the student usually won't do that, but they'll do just about everything else. We go around and troubleshoot rather than lead like a lead carpenter." [Steve]

CLOTHING

Clothing is a key tool for safety, which OSHA calls "personal protective equipment," or PPE. Soft hats provide sun protection, and hard hats safeguard design/builders when construction is overhead or objects might fall from above. Safety glasses protect eyes from wood chips and other airborne objects when sawing, hammering, and cutting. Respirators mitigate dust and fibers while cleaning or demolishing on a project's site. Gloves guard against blisters. Work pants help prevent inadvertent scrapes, cuts, and bruises. Sturdy shoes should substitute for open-toe footwear.

COMMUNICATION

Communication and interaction on the jobsite is another important safety factor. At Yestermorrow Steve notes how the closeness of students and instructors reduces the project's pitfalls, and the best practice is "to do a responsible job, avoid dangerous situations, and supervise very closely." More specifically, Steve adds that if "there's a really potentially hairy cut, generally one of us will take it." From the instructor's perspective, it is necessary to watch out for students who are not comfortable with a particular task as well as students who "think they can do it and just can't."

SHOP

Shops are where things are made. A school's shop facilities certainly offer resources for a design/build studio—welding, metalwork, and woodwork. **Fig. 80** But Jim has pointed out the advantages of being independent: it helps to build an inventory of tools dedicated to design/build work and keep them in a storage container that can serve both on campus and on jobsites. Steve sets up his own shop in the yard and interior spaces of the studio's Community Design Building. This arrangement maximizes flexibility and mirrors what they will use on the jobsite. When on-site construction begins, the tools are mobilized and relocated to the site: "This is essentially the setup most contractors use on site, when there are no shop facilities available." Steve typically rents a Mobile-Mini container, along with a security fence, for secure storage of tools and materials on the site. **Figs. 81–82**

Fig. 80 University of Washington metal shop during project for Wellspring.

MOBILE SHOP

Steve's setup on site and in the Community Design Building's yard includes a sliding compound miter saw mounted on a stand with work stops and supports and a beam that extends to support 16-foot material. The studio also uses a Rousseau bench-top table saw stand that accepts various brands of portable table saws and folds down for storage or transport.

Fig. 81 Double bevel sliding compound miter saw with legstand.

Fig. 82 Portable table saw with Rousseau outfeed tables.

On the University of Miami campus, Jim and Rocco set up outside the architecture building under tarpaulins; and the current plan calls a new 36-by-36-foot open-air workshop that will house the studio and offer "plenty of daylight, layout space, tool storage, and a sliding crane" to lift the project onto delivery trucks. **Fig. 83** This setup allows for substantial off-site, in-house construction and—typical of prefabrication approaches—can improve quality control and avoid weather delays. Jim notes the advantages of prefab, comparing the University of Miami studio to the model at Yestermorrow, "where we build the project at the shop and then transport it to a site. In the two-week time period, we just couldn't build something in situ because it would take so much time getting back and forth between the school and the site. The whole of studio time would be taken up in travel, and then setting up and breaking down tools." **Fig. 84** One disadvantage is that the project is limited in size to what can be transported on roadways (but this constraint can also be a positive factor—see "Scope" in "Groundwork"). Prefabrication can also occur in temporary, or case-by-case, facilities. In Steve's Beacon Food Forest project, the studio used the hangar space at Sand Point Naval Air Station as an ad hoc shop to fabricate and assemble the component parts—"It was definitely efficient, particularly in a rainy climate like Seattle." **Fig. 85**

Fig. 83 Design/build work area at University of Miami.

Fig. 84 Students working in the shaded area of the outdoor yard at Yestermorrow, 2013.

Fig. 85 Jake LaBarre (center), who coteaches with Steve at the University of Washington, talks with students about the Beacon Food Forest project at the Sand Point facility, 2013.

In other situations, the shop *is* the studio. With Jim and Steve's Public Interest Design/Build studio, Yestermorrow's facilities include a small classroom bracketed by a covered outdoor builder's yard on one side and a full shop on the other. This proximity allows for a dynamic interchange between discussing and presenting designs and actually making things—components in the shop and assemblies in the yard. Here, integrated spaces of design and build counter the drawbacks of two separate education spaces: shop and studio.

Fig. 86 Jim's studio constructed the Motes Orchid Pavilion in three separate pieces, and then spent two days (back-to-back) transporting components to the site.

At the University of Miami, the tarpaulin canopy that shelters the temporary design/build shop occupies an outdoor space formed by the L shape of the School of Architecture's buildings. Adjacent to the model shop and furniture design studio, it offers ready access to the school's other spaces. From the second floor, other design studios can watch the design/build progress. The open-air workshop also occupies a highly visible public space where members of the "university community stop and talk about what is going on." Not relegated to a basement or peripheral outbuilding, this shop creates a sense of community, and design/build is its culture. **Fig. 86**

Shop managers are invaluable resources for a design/build studio. Jim tells a story highlighting the insights of the University of Miami's manager, Adrian Alfonso Villaraos:

"The knowledge of the shop manager is always important. When we built the pavilion for Motes Orchids, it was made up of three sections, and they were each really heavy. We had to transport them down to the site, but first we had to get them up onto this lowboy trailer. Adrian, the shop manager, said that back in Cuba, when they had to move heavy cargo, they would just get a bunch of oranges. And we were confused. So he told us to get some oranges and he'd show us how to move this thing. We cut a couple of dozen oranges in half. Of course, the first thing you have to do, he said, is eat the oranges. The students ate the oranges [*laughs*], and then we put the rinds down on the ramped skids that we were pushing this pavilion up on and 'swish'—it slid right up onto the truck… with us pushing. It's the oil in the orange peels. Adrian said he used to move around heavy equipment that way back in Cuba." **Figs. 87-91**

Figs. 87–90 "So he said, 'Get some oranges and I'll show you how to move this thing.'"—Jim's story about a shop manager.

Fig. 91 Students with one of the components of the Motes Orchid Pavilion ready for transport to the site, 2009.

JOBSITE

There is also much to be learned from life on the jobsite, a place that tends to emphasize building as a social enterprise. Passersby observe, clients stop in, weather changes, and students get out into the community.

"A lot of our projects are in community gardens and there's often a landscape component, so it's nice to be out on the site. The fact that we didn't have a dedicated shop for so long means that everyone learned how to work out of the back of a truck like a typical contractor does." [Steve]

Site-built construction increases participants' connections to community and context—and, as Steve suggests, to the landscape itself. **Fig. 92** Working on site connects with local residents while fostering community among those who are building the project. Recollection of a Jersey Devil jobsite rings true for today's design/build studios.

SB: On the Silo House jobsite, we had a pretty cool thing, a ritualistic lunch program. We'd all cut up 2x4s and start a fire.

JA: It was a social environment—you get to know the people you're working with. It becomes a family, more than just a jobsite. That's the ethos that I remember. At one point, we were shingling with cedar, and there were a lot of off-cuts from the shingles. Along with scrap 2x4s, those were the kindling to get the fire started. Tom Galbraith would be the chef, and we'd cook outside on a couple of cinder blocks where we put a grill down. The cook-up was a big deal. John Kemp got some urethane foam, and with the overspraying, he made a gigantic hat, and after he put on a robe, he would ceremoniously come up for his hot dog. And the old trick was cooking our hamburgers on printers' plates...

SB: Tom thought that was a good idea...over the fire...

JR: On aluminum plates?

SB: Bad idea. The best was when we nailed him to the deck when he was sleeping. Tom was considered an old guy on the site. He was forty...like this geezer we had working with us.

JA: We nailed the cuff of his pants to the floor and then woke him up . . . the tricks you play on forty-year-olds...

JR: ...geezers...

SB: He was fabulous...he had the big gray beard...he might have looked older than he was, but forty seemed ancient at the time.

JR: I remember sometimes it seemed like we'd have a discussion, just brainstorming nonsense—it had nothing necessarily to do with the job—but you'd say something and then, oh, that's the idea, that's a million-dollar idea—let's get back to work. This feeling that you had a freeform discussion, inventions of silliness.

(Steve says that Tom Galbraith was "a great inspiration to all of us in his lifelong commitment to art and making things, even when he was hobbling around on feet he fabricated in his shop." Jersey Devil was using the aluminum printers' plates for the Silo House's solar collector.)

Such experiences on site stick with you (Steve recalls that the plates eventually caught fire and the burgers fell into the coals). To hear Jim, Steve, and John talk about these experiences is to be back, forty years ago, at the Silo House with them in the place, a part of the ritual, the lunch program, and each vibrant workday, pranks and all.

The site—its events, actors, tricks, chats—and its physical presence all contribute to the process of building. You're right there and it's around you. Now get back to work!

Fig. 92 Formwork for steps at Steve's 2007 project for Danny Woo Community Garden. The project involved grading and re-grading the site, laying out paths, and applying surface treatments like gravel, flagstone, and tumbled glass.

PROCESS

START TO FINISH

Design/build is a living process that occurs in real time, with a physical presence and an immediate context. You choose a project to develop and it takes on its own life. From start to finish—and finish you must—this process intertwines practical logistics with pedagogical goals. From day one, phasing and framing the project come together in a rich—and sometimes daunting— cascade of learning objectives, technical limitations, facility requirements, site constraints, and group dynamics. Education contends with training, and in fostering that learning, process is key. **Figs. 01–02**

Fig. 01 Time-lapse photographs of Helping Link Community Center project in Seattle, 2010.

Fig. 02 Ribbon cutting at the Helping Link Community Center.

This chapter takes the design/build project through its process, from start to finish. How does the process unfold during the project itself? And what needs to happen afterward? Design/build's process works progressively and iteratively. In the former, each new step builds on the preceding step and moves toward the goal of completion; in the latter, repetition refines ideas and develops skills. Small-group charrettes cycle and recycle design concepts toward a consensus of the larger group, and countless chop saw cuts hone the coordination of eye, measurement, blade alignment, and material.

In teaching design/build, one must plan for an array of activities and learning outcomes: working in groups, designing at a rapid pace, learning tools and techniques, selecting and procuring materials, and meeting with clients—all of this while completing the project on time. Jim and Steve's overall rule of thumb for scheduling the studio term is one-third design and two-thirds build. This section focuses on the process of teaching—and learning—from the beginning of the term to the punch list and finishing party.

INSTRUCTORS

Steve points out that design/build instructors must be aware of everything, even if it's beyond their field of vision, and he adds, "Somebody who has a family is usually pretty good at this." He prefers to teach with at least one other instructor and one work-study student who has construction experience. A greater number of instructors allows increased supervision on the jobsite, a wider range of experience, and, in turn, more feedback within the studio. At Yestermorrow, three instructors teach the Public Interest Design/Build studio, typically providing a faculty to student ratio of one to four.

" **Design/build instructors should have eyes in the back of their heads.**" [Steve]

An important feedback aspect is the relation between instructor and assistant, which is not unlike the journeyman system within craft's mentor-mentee traditions. Yestermorrow Design/Build School has established an intern system that typically adds one or two advanced students to Jim and Steve's studio. Steve notes that this is "like having teaching assistants who know the ropes, the shop, the tools, the protocol." Additional instructors can also help with logistics: scheduling, preparing drawings if they need to be permitted, and crafting presentations. In one case at the University of Washington, a work-study student developed a bookkeeping system and template for the Neighborhood Design/Build Studio.

Overall, these studios provide a forum for intensive pedagogy and exemplary team teaching. Design/build instructors are educators, facilitators, and editors—as John says, "We're here to show them how we discover and resolve issues." **Fig. 03** At Yestermorrow, the daily close interaction between students and instructors allows for a learning environment where talking and building twine together to create lively workshops—more discussion than debate but lively nonetheless: "If we have a misunderstanding or a disagreement, that's a teachable moment. There are no secrets at Yestermorrow. What do you think? What should we do here? How are we going to solve this? Well, this is what I would do. What would you do? That's a productive discussion, and the students are witness to it." As editors, instructors help students refine often overstuffed projects in the design phase and continue to revise details and joints once construction has started. They must also be ready to look for design opportunities in unlikely places.

Jim, John, and Steve have many stories of how instructors' tolerance relates to design opportunities:

Fig. 03 John oversees a student cutting purlins for the firewood and garden shed project during his Home Design/Build course, 2011.

JA: You have to be tolerant and understanding with the students. You know they started cutting the floor joists, and they were too short so we—

SB: shortened the floor?

JA: So, we shortened the floor...

JR: A design opportunity to shorten the floor, right?

DAY ONE

Steve calls this the "most fun day" of the term (even though he tends to say that almost every day). There are many transitions on the first day: into a new class, from traditional studio into a design/build format, from what students know into what they don't know. Familiar spaces and common materials can inform these transitions. John's studio at Yestermorrow includes nonarchitecture students, so on the first day he asks everyone to draw their dormitory rooms. With measuring and drawing to introduce the activity of building, students make connections between their living space, its representation, its volumes, and their composition.

DESIGN/BUILD STUDIO QUESTIONNAIRE

Jim and Rocco Ceo ask their design/build studios to fill out a questionnaire on the first day of class:

1. What is/are your reason(s) for taking the design/build studio?
2. Prior to signing up for this studio, how much building experience have you had? Be specific.
3. What do you imagine will be the primary benefit of this studio experience for your future career as an architect?
4. Irrespective of your future status as an architect, what do you perceive to be the primary benefit of design/build to you personally?
5. What aspect of design/build do you anticipate will be the most difficult?
6. What aspect of design/build do you anticipate will be the easiest?
7. Please describe what you believe are your best skills as a designer.

With a class made up entirely of architecture and building construction students, Steve and Jim begin to design and build right away. Jim's first such exercise is for students to draw a caricature of themselves when they sign in on day one. Jim starts this process with his own quick sketch. Rocco compiled a questionnaire that he and Jim distribute in order to understand student goals and expertise.

For his studio, Steve says, "We talk about who we are and what experience we have building…and then we build some things." They begin with ordinary letter-sized sheets of paper (8½ by 11 inches), simple operations (stretch and fold), and uncomplicated technologies (tape and staple). They ask: How strong is paper? What is a sheet of paper's structural potential?

"We give them a sheet of letter-sized paper and ask them to describe it, and they'll usually say it's flimsy. But if you hold one end of it and I hold the other end of it, it's really impossible to tear—so it's really strong in tension. Then I fold it, and we put a pencil on it to show that it'll take compression if you configure it differently. Next I ask them to build a bridge. With suspension bridges, we've had 50-foot spans. And then they build a tower. They have a great time building, and these exercises introduce them to compression and tension. They start making stuff right away. The bridge can use paper and staples, and the tower can use paper and tape…. And then there's a take-home problem where they build a 4-inch-high foundation. We test that to failure, which is really amazing, because it holds concrete blocks or even a huge stack of books, which is fun." [Steve]

The resulting bridges and towers—each designed, built, and tested in about forty-five minutes—make for a lively, performative first class that sets up the idea of the studio as a builder's yard for experimentation.

Figs. 04–05 Paper Bridge and Tower exercises, Neighborhood Design/Build Studio, University of Washington, 2010.

DAY ONE EXERCISES
(derived from Steve and Jim's handouts)

Paper Bridge Project
PROBLEM

Using only one sheet of 8 ½-by-11-inch paper and metal staples, build a bridge that spans the longest possible distance.

LIMITATIONS
→ Time limit for construction is twenty minutes.
→ Bridge cannot be stapled to any surface.
→ Bridge must span the distance unsupported.

Paper Tower Project
PROBLEM

Using only one sheet of 8 ½-by-11-inch paper and scotch tape, build the tallest possible vertical structure that stands on flat surfaces.

LIMITATIONS
→ Time limit for construction is twenty minutes.
→ Tower must be freestanding.
→ Tape must be used sparingly.

Paper Foundation Project
PROBLEM

Using only one sheet of 8 ½-by-11-inch paper and white glue, construct a foundation that will support as much weight as possible.

LIMITATIONS
→ Time limit for construction is twenty minutes.
→ Foundation must be at least four inches tall.
→ Foundation can dry for twenty-four hours.

RECORDS FROM PAPER EXERCISES

Jim's Studios:
JIM NOTES: "The paper exercises provide a really fun and participatory atmosphere. Students are amazed at how tall a paper tower can stand freely and how long a bridge can span."

BRIDGE: 58 feet: "At University of Miami, the studio is a series of 12-by-30-foot rooms with central doors that provide a connecting hallway when opened. As the bridges stretch out, students are shocked as door after door needs to be opened—sometimes through other studios. Once, the bridge exited the building."

TOWER: 74 inches

FOUNDATION (COMPRESSION MODELS WITHOUT GLUE): 22 pounds

Steve's Studios:
BRIDGE: Longest typically between 50 and 60 feet. Steve recalls one that was 96 feet, built by a student with "incredible eye/hand skills who could cut the paper into one 1/16" strip—we had to take it outside to stretch it out. The point is to make a suspension bridge, using the paper in tension; staples aren't really required for the solution."

TOWER: Typically in the 6-foot range. One of the towers reached eight feet: "The good ones usually do an Eiffel Tower–type structure...This one was amazing!"

FOUNDATION (WITH GLUE): 50 pounds

On the first morning of his Home Design/Build course at Yestermorrow, John lays his tool belt on the desk and unrolls a long sheet of utility paper on the floor. He cuts the end of the sheet, pulls out a measuring tape from the belt, and asks his students to help him measure and mark distances on the paper.

With help from each student in turn, John stretches and pops a chalk line to form a linework grid: 6-inch rows alternate with 3-inch rows across the 36-inch width, and 12-inch columns divide the paper's length.

The full-scale page is a combination of lined and graph paper writ large. In 1990, when John was first asked to teach at Yestermorrow, he felt like he needed something to organize his thoughts and introduce his students to his experience with design/build. He wanted to talk with the students as if they were already building and already on the jobsite. For John, this paper becomes a construction site, where we speak with tools at hand. The drawing demonstrates the making of design/build.

John begins writing on the sheet and spells out "D-E-S-I-G-N" at the top left. He says this is the ideal location for design, at the beginning, but if you look around our built environment, you will find that most of it is not actually designed first. Design, he notes, is about clear intentions and finding delight, pleasure, and beauty while simultaneously solving problems. To the right, he pens "B-U-I-L-D."

After a pause, he adds a forward slash between the two words. "It's all one process." He says *making* is the word that best describes this "bind" between design and build. For John, this process is magic.

He elaborates:

"If I were to pull a rabbit out of a hat, you would say it's magic. In design/build, we also start with absolutely nothing and end with something real and tangible. From nothing to something… magic. How do we make choices that engage this magic? In design/build projects, we confront many, many decisions. This can be daunting, but there are two things that make it possible: First, given the right input, you are wired to make decisions. Then if you are clear about your intentions in the design phase, you will have a guidebook during the construction phase. The purpose of this drawing and this class is to distill that process. It is not a recipe but a guide, a wayfinding handbook. Feedback helps.

MEDIA: 36-by-96-inch (or similar size) sheet of white utility paper
TOOLS: utility knife, measuring tapes, chalk line, straight edge, markers
TIME: about thirty minutes

At breakfast this morning, you made your sandwich for lunch [a tradition at Yestermorrow]. With all the choices of breads, fillings, and condiments, there might have been a thousand possible sandwiches on the table. Yet you all made lunch without being overwhelmed. You harnessed your innate ability to make decisions. We're wired to do this. In the studio, we will build an awareness of this decision-making process and help clarify your design intentions to achieve the finished project."

While he explains these ideas, John has outlined both "design" and "build" in red. He then draws arrows to illustrate three main feedback loops. From the end of build to the start of design, from the slash back to design, and then from build forward to the slash.

"The key concept here is that the design/build process is *not* linear—even if we wish it were. It is full of feedback loops, and we have to embrace that feedback by expecting it and realizing that when we have to loop back we are doing the design/build process. We are learning and refining as the project takes shape. This will continue until we are done with the project and even after that."

John then begins again, working from left to right on the next line, to highlight four design phases and four build phases. *Dream, Decide, Develop, Document* on the design side, and then *Decipher, Delegate, Do, Done* on the build side. *Dream*: For the first couple of days, John will ask students to turn off their editor and allow ideas, good and bad, to flow.

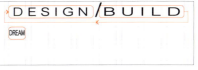

Many of his students are new to the design process, so he cultivates an atmosphere where "there are no wrong answers" and rethinking is a natural part of decision-making, integral to feedback. With sketches and models, he helps students make their "verbal dreams visual."

Decide: On day three in studio, John will ask his students to "put their editor on." Feedback starts in earnest. Design ideas meet with edits, accountability, and hybrid decision making. *Develop*: As the afternoon build sessions gain momentum in days four and five, John's students consider the actual implications of what they are designing and representing.

Document: "Construction is about communication," he says. Here John also discusses design communication, and how the students will work from schematic to more detailed drawings and eventually to a physical model at ¼" = 1'-0".

John then points to the slash:

"When we have documented our project, we have created pictures and words describing what it wants to be, and we've reached a stage not unlike the 'pretty pictures' in the center of a cookbook. But it is not a recipe of how to make the pictures come alive. To do that, we need to move into the build phase. In the traditional arrangement, the architect will hand off the drawings to the builder, who has to figure out what the pictures are showing and then figure out a recipe for making it. That is a very valuable talent and one that should not be underestimated. What makes the design/build process different is right at this slash. If the designer is the builder, there is an economy of communication at this moment. Knowing how to build improves design, and knowing how to design improves build."

In this part of the conversation, John has been tracking the feedback loops between each successive concept.

Decipher: Now, under B-U-I-L-D, he continues to discuss communication and the translation of design to build, comments on costing materials, and notes the variability in building estimates. Also, remember that the "dream will keep giving you guidance," even as practicalities grow.

Delegate: Find competent people. John's advice speaks to designs you're self-building and to those that you contract out.

Do: Finally, you're doing it.

"The project is taking physical shape and, after all this time and preparation, we still need to refer back to our original intentions. Materials you want may be unavailable or too expensive. A detail you were developing might not work as planned. Any number of contingencies might demand you check back to your dream and make minor adaptations or alterations. That is the fun and excitement of building, and that is what we'll be doing each afternoon as we work on our class construction project."

Dream: John's loops have periodically streamed back to the starting point—the original vision keeps feeding back in at every stage.

Done: This point is different for everyone. Each person has different dones. But there is a common outcome of completion.

"Finally we get to 'Done' in our project. Done, unfortunately, is not so simple to define. Done for the plumber might not be done for the building inspector or the banker or the homeowner. The main point is to be clear when you start with each person about what is expected and what the definition of *done* will be for their part of the work. Even here, there is going to be feedback."

DESIGN				/BUILD			
DREAM	DECIDE	DEVELOP	DOCUMENT	DECIPHER	DELEGATE	DO	DONE
PRE-DESIGN & SITE ANALYSIS	SCHEMATIC DESIGN	DESIGN DEVELOPMENT	CONSTRUCTION DOCUMENTS	BID PROJECT	CONTRACT PROJECT	CONSTRUCT PROJECT	COMPLETE PROJECT

In a later conversation with John about this process, I realize halfway through that he hasn't been looking at the image of the poster I've pulled up on my computer screen. He works entirely from memory. The image—and its rich connotations—are in his head. And in the studio, when he makes the drawing, it is not delivered as a lecture, but instead an exercise in talking and doing. It resides in the slash; it is about making.

The result is a drawing of design/build to illustrate the process, some of its tools, and the interaction—physical movement as well as collaborative dialogue—that will make up the studio. When you enter John's Home Design/Build studio on Yestermorrow's second floor, the completed banner floats above the room's work space and reminds us of design/ build's foundational process. **Fig. 06** After the overview of the design/build concept, on this first morning of his class, John demonstrates more drawing basics, talks about how to read plans and scale drawings, and assigns the exercise to draw their dormitory rooms and hands out the detailed schedule for the two week class.

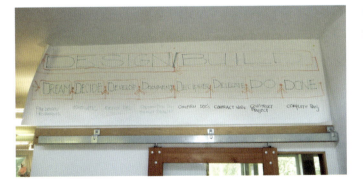

Fig. 06 John's design/ build drawing posted in the Yestermorrow studio, 2013.

WEEK ONE

For Steve's second day of class, students bring in their 4-inch-high paper foundations for testing. Here Sweets catalogs—if you can still find them—serve as vibrant and solid units to load the paper to failure. **Fig. 07** Steve surprises students with the capacity of their foundations to hold concrete blocks. He follows the paper exercises with an assignment asking students to design and build an object of their choice out of a single sheet of ¼" plywood and an 8-foot 2x4, or a half sheet of ¼" plywood and a 4-foot 2x4. Quickly moving from sheets of paper to sheets of plywood, students receive the exercise on the first day and, on day two, bring in preliminary drawings that are discussed after the foundation tests. In order "to fast-track it," Jim no longer assigns this exercise and instead asks students to design a pair of sawhorses.

Both Steve and Jim conduct the group consensus exercise during the first few classes before design begins. [see "Consensus" in "Toolbox"] By the end of the first week or the beginning of the second, they will have asked students to begin materials research and design scheme proposals. The first week also includes initial discussions of what will be built, site visits and analysis, and a preliminary meeting with clients, which often occurs on the second day of class.

Fig. 07 Paper Foundation exercises, Neighborhood Design/ Build Studio, University of Washington, 2010.

WOOD EXERCISE: PLYWOOD AND 2X4

Problem:
Design and build an object of your choice from a half or full sheet of ¼" plywood and one 8-foot 2x4. Consider the form, strength and workability of these materials and aim for the minimum waste and efficient layout.

Drawing:
The first effort will be devoted to generating an idea and producing design drawings, sketches, and models. Before beginning construction, legible, dimensioned working drawings at an appropriate scale must be completed: plan, sections, elevations, and details (including sheet layout). Edits and additions to the object are acceptable as long as they incorporate the original design concepts.

Requirements:
→ Design sketches due before class Wednesday
→ Working drawings due Friday
→ Finished piece due Monday at the beginning of class; informal review of work
→ Documentation

Fig. 08 Plywood project from University of Washington design/build studio, 2007.

Fig. 09 Plywood project from University of Washington design/build studio, 2007.

Fig. 10 Plywood projects from University of Washington design/build studio, 2010.

Fig. 11 Studio review of solar oven project from plywood exercise during University of Miami design/build studio, 2010.

Fig. 12 Solar oven project and wine-glass rack, University of Miami design/build studio, 2010.

SAWHORSE

During the first week, Jim asks students to design a pair of sawhorses. Three construction requirements guide the students' work: four feet long, thirty inches tall, and stackable. Jim encourages students to use standard material stock: 1x6, 2x6, or 2x4. As an alternative, he also challenges a few students to build the sawhorses out of one sheet of ¾" plywood. Jim asks students to avoid internet resources—there are many designs available—because he wants students to explore relationships between function and art.

Originally, Jim thought the sawhorse construction project would provide a context for introducing tools, but in practice he has found that building sawhorses can also fill gaps in the construction schedule or otherwise idle times when one group of students is waiting for another group to complete a task. "Let's build that set of sawhorses you designed earlier in the semester" becomes the call to work.

Fig. 13 Sawhorses from Jim and Rocco's 2014 design/build studio.

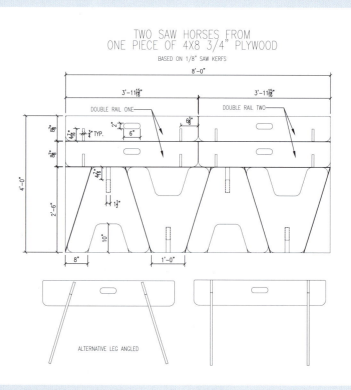

Fig. 14 Jim's plans for a sawhorse.

GROUP

If we really want to build something cool, then maybe I should just design it and the class can build it." Steve's proposal gets the attention of his students. Some puzzled, others indignant. "Whoa, whoa, wait a minute. So if it's not OK for me to design it, then why would we pick your scheme or your scheme or your scheme?

Once the project description has been introduced, Jim and Steve follow the consensus exercise with short discussions—modeled on architectural charrettes—to achieve studio consensus on a design scheme. They divide students evenly into teams. Steve likes to begin with three teams to expedite presentations, but depending on the overall number, the groups might also be smaller—four teams of three or four, or five teams of three.

After thirty to forty-five minutes, each group presents its proposed design scheme to the rest of the studio. Jim and Steve then shuffle the members and ask the new teams to repeat the process. Changing groups creates what Jim calls the "joint experience of investigating." Good ideas come to the surface, and bad ideas are sifted out. And the danger of a single controlling faction or dominant individual is avoided. During this process, Steve also modifies the program to include common features of previous schemes. With the refinement of design ideas and as the schemes move closer together, subgroups can grow larger, progressing toward a group that is the studio itself.

Jim and Steve do not allow voting in this group process. Consequently, debates must always be resolved with discussion. In the Coffee Kiosk project, studio discussion came down to two schemes: what Jim and Rocco called the Lincoln Log group and the louvered lantern group. **Figs. 15–16** After repeated shuffling of students into different groups, the studio reached an impasse with the two schemes. At the sixth meeting, each student was asked to speak

Fig. 15 Model of the "Lincoln log" group's proposal for the Coffee Kiosk, University of Miami's design/build studio, 2014.

Fig. 16 The "louvered lantern" group discusses their design for the Coffee Kiosk project, University of Miami's design/build studio, 2014.

about the pros and cons of the schemes, with a particular emphasis on the practicality of their design and construction. Issues like waterproofing, longevity, and maintenance yielded a consensus decision for the lantern scheme.

It is also possible for individual projects to prepare students for group work. Steve's plywood exercise shows the studio how many unique responses are possible from the same starting point (a single sheet of plywood). And when John led off Jersey Devil's joint design/build studio at the University of Wisconsin, he began studio with a series of short, often weeklong, individual projects that then phased into a group project. This sequence helped students make the transition from drawing to building and from individual to collaborative work. John found that there "were a lot of lessons that each student learned individually," which prepared students for questions such as, "You might be able to draw it, but how do you build it?" And, eventually, how do you build it as a group?

After the studio reaches consensus about the design scheme, groups take on more in-depth investigations of particular components and systems. These tasks can be self-selected so the design development phase often plays to students' strengths. Preparation for the start of construction can include additional study models, drawing sets, development of structural components, and further site analysis. **Figs. 17–18**

Similar to shuffling group members in the design process, allowing students to shuffle between tasks during construction cultivates full collaboration throughout the build process. Instructors can facilitate participation, and Jim has remarked that he is constantly "switching people out" to make sure each student is exposed to as many different situations—tools, methods, and site conditions—as possible. This process avoids pigeonholing, which is often cited as a negative aspect in the discussion of group work.

Repetitive tasks also allow for group involvement in the early stages of instruction. Learning how to use a tool can become a group activity in which each student has a chance to perform the task. Cutting sheets of plywood on the site is a good process for teaching how to use the circular saw. Thin sheets of plywood laid across support boards on sawhorses allow the saw blade to be set shallower, teaching the setup of depth adjustments and easing the minds of students who are wary of the saw's power and torque. Students can also see how the rotation of the blade affects the finish of the cut, often splintering the top and cutting more cleanly along the bottom. In the various sheds for his Home Design/Build studio, John has used a similar process of cutting kerfs (for metal braces) across the vertical studs to introduce the circular saw. For each new tool, John begins this process with a call for volunteers and then works with each student so that the tool is familiar to all.

Fig. 17 Typical corner condition of the Coffee Kiosk project, 2014.

Fig. 18 The cantilevered corner in the Coffee Kiosk project came out of group discussions about structure, light, and joints.

Fig. 19 Steve and John discuss the 2013 Home Design/Build outbuilding project.

SB: You have to watch out for what we call pigeon-holing, which is when somebody does a job and does it well, and that's all he or she ends up doing…the person who does the planing or the person who operates the table saw. Pigeonholing— getting slotted into one job—is usually one of the things on the list that students cite as a negative. I work with construction management students who are often dual majors, and they get pigeonholed because the architecture students appear to be genetically incapable of putting together a materials take-off, a budget, or a schedule.

JA: So our job is to make sure everybody participates in each part of the process, whether it be roofing, framing, or working in the shop…We're always switching people out.

SB: Early on, we have a meeting to talk about who can do what. As we're building, the teachers are going around, watching and correcting and helping as well as teaching tricks for construction. It's a class within the class. We troubleshoot rather than lead like a lead carpenter does.

JR: My studio is a little different. I'm always calling for volunteers. First we'll explain why we are putting a brace into the wall and we'll discuss that it requires what's called a "depth cut." Typically, nobody in the group has ever used a circular saw for a depth cut. We'll use the chalk box to make the cut line, and we'll make sure everybody knows about setting depths on the saw. Then I'll ask for a volunteer. There's a lot of silence, and then somebody will step forward, and after three studs, we'll ask for another volunteer. Eventually, we get across the whole wall. And everybody has had a hands-on experience with the circular saw, learning to make a depth cut.

SB: Maybe pick three different studs… **Fig. 19**

JR: We have a blue line struck where we're going to cut, so somebody will do three studs, somebody else will do three more, etc.

SB: I see why it takes so long to build those things.

TYPICAL DAY

Design/build studio classes begin and end with meetings to help "keep everyone on track." During construction the crew rolls out the tools and then comes together for a short meeting to itemize the work, assign tasks, and talk about longer-term goals. Once the tools are rolled up, the studio meets again to organize and prepare for the next class. In Steve's studio, each meeting ends with the slow clap and a cheer.

"In the design/build groups, there's a lot of communication that goes on. We have a meeting at the beginning of the class where we talk about all the tasks that need to be done and who's going to do them, and then we have another one at the end after we roll up. And after every class, we have this thing that we do at Yestermorrow and University of Washington, where everybody claps. We start out with a slow clap that gets faster and faster and then everybody cheers, which is reminiscent of a sort of Walmart sales meeting or something like that, but we love it. And after a while, you think you're just going home without doing it, and everybody says hey, we can't go—we haven't clapped yet." [Steve] **Fig. 20**

Fig. 20 Steve leads group claps during the 2009 studio and at the dedication of the 2011 design/build project.

At the University of Washington, classes meet three times in the afternoon during the week for five hours (12:30 to 5:30 PM) and again on Saturday from 10 am to 2 PM, followed by an after-work cookout organized by a rotating group of students. Jim's studio at Miami meets twice a week from 1:30 PM to 6 PM. At Yestermorrow, two-week courses start right after breakfast and continue into the evening.

The typical day in Jim and Steve's Yestermorrow design/build class meshes design and build within an intense schedule and the shared physical spaces of studio and shop. The classroom connects directly to the workshop and outdoor building yard, and Steve and Jim joke about how they like to slide between spaces, rolling and pointing in their wheeled chairs. Each day begins with a group meeting in the classroom to divide up construction tasks throughout the main building's linked spaces. In his class at Yestermorrow, John breaks the class day into three sessions. Students work in the design

REPETITION: ITERATIVE APPROACHES AND RECURRENT OPERATIONS

→ laying trace over a schematic design proposal

→ crafting a study model

→ shuffling groups in a design charrette

→ making cuts with circular saws, chop saws, table saws, and pull-stroke hand saws

→ screwing down boards

→ using a jig for repeated construction components

→ planing rough-sawn boards

→ scribing a joist, rafter, or truss layout

studio in the morning from about 8 AM until noon, and then again in the evening after dinner; they build in the afternoon from 1 PM to 5 PM. In nine four-hour afternoon sessions, John's class frames up a small outbuilding or garden shed and typically adds sheathing and roofing before the course's completion.

Steve believes that design/build is a uniquely iterative process. In studio, we draw and redraw and revisit design schemes, while also forming and re-forming groups to reach consensus. In the shop and on the construction site, we repeat cuts and fasten standardized joints. Repetition works, but it takes time, and time is certainly a limiting factor, yet choreographing these iterative operations fosters collaboration as it also builds confidence. What Steve calls "replicable experiences" cycle through a design/build project and float within the process like aggregate in cement.

" **Construction is all about 'do it; now do it again; do it again; do it again.'** " [John]

REVIEW AND CRITIQUE

You cannot hide in design/build work. Participation is a highly visible process—you're either there or you're not, and you're either working or you're standing around. Full scale equates to full exposure. Details and joints, fit and functionality are all available for inspection. In contrast to other studio work in which tools of representation might be used to obscure design results, design/build production opens itself to critique. Design critics become users, stand-ins for clients, who can test results firsthand.

Early in the design process, Steve moves through group discussions and design charrettes to provide "reality checks" on student proposals. This commentary targets not only buildability but also how the actual grounds the conceptual. Students may not realize it at the time, but these critiques prepare them for the realities of full-scale construction.

SCHEDULE

To maintain a schedule that is one-third design and two-thirds construction requires harnessing group dynamics, finding a typical daily rhythm, and assessing progress on a daily basis. On the quarter system, University of Washington's eleven-week terms mean three or four weeks of design and seven or eight of construction. The University of Miami's sixteen-week semesters provide a little more than five weeks for designing and slightly less than eleven for building. And Yestermorrow's concentrated two-week schedule makes for three days of design and eight or nine for construction, but Jim and Steve try to push for design resolution in the first two days to allow more time for building, and John's course relies on nine four-hour sessions to build as much as possible by the end of the course.

Before classes start, Steve schedules a meeting with clients for Monday of the third week. Students contend with this fixed date and make adjustments to stay on schedule. He notes that the studio typically finds consensus by the end of the second week and uses the weekend to prepare for the presentation. John's course schedule tracks daily activities as it also helps visualize a curriculum that relies on feedback between design and build. Drafting in the studio parallels surveying and site mapping on the construction site. A morning lesson on budgeting often lines up with the arrival of the construction project's materials. Part of his teaching and the students' educational experience is the idea that they all participate in the schedule. John acknowledges at the outset that it will be a working document.

SCHEDULING

Design/build can introduce students to construction scheduling models such as Gantt charts and the Critical Path Method (CPM), with their milestones and job paths. CPM addresses the complex, multifaceted process of construction by creating a network of activities, which are linked to those that follow. The critical path is the networked chain of activities with the longest duration—delay one of these critical activities and you will delay the project. Gantt charts illustrate the start to finish schedule of activities in a bar chart. Gantts are bar charts that graph specific activities according to time—from start to finish; they clearly portray the overlaps of activities. In the end, the studio's schedule and educational objectives mean that the class must tailor its essential organization to pedagogical objectives (visualized in John's matrix schedule), and it must also be responsive to changes on a case-by-case basis to allow for fast or slow pacing.

"There are many programs these days that will help compute the materials and calculate the budget, and they always generate those bar charts. Gantt charts should be called 'can't charts.' Often the first thing we talk about at the meeting is how far behind schedule we are. We always finish on time and on budget, hopefully because the instructors have selected the right scope of the project and have been carefully working with the client before the class even starts." [Steve]

JOB LOG

Jim has recently begun keeping a job log that includes handwritten notes, sketches, typed records of daily activities, receipts, research materials, and other project specifications. This document pulls together disparate activities, from design deliberations to alternate details to results from the bridge, tower, and foundation exercises. It serves as a vital archive of the process and a useful reference for future projects.

WEEKLY SCHEDULE: WEEK-BY-WEEK ACCOMPLISHMENTS DURING STEVE'S NOJI COMMONS PROJECT IN 2004
(adapted from student project booklet)

Completed in 2004 in Seattle's Rainier Valley district, Noji Gardens subdivision includes affordable single-family homes and town homes developed by the nonprofit group HomeSight and sold to first-time homebuyers. Two years later, the design/build project transformed the development's cul-de-sac traffic circle into a community gathering space.

The class included the following: Steve Badanes (professor), Damon Smith (instructor), Erin Sonntag and Laurie Stallings (authors of the booklet), Cedric Barringer, Dave Biddle, Jacqueline Bui, Tim Carter, David Cheifetz, Mike Freeman, Mark Haizlip, Zach Ham, Richard Jackman, John Kirk, Morgan McIntosh, Ryan Peck, Yevgenia Podvysotska, Greg Squires, Sam Batchellor (teaching assistant), Molly Cherney (teaching assistant), Craig Hollow (teaching assistant), and Kari Callahan (volunteer).

Week One

→ Completed paper exercises (bridge, tower, and foundation)
→ Visited site
→ Met with community members to generate program wish list and preliminary design scheme
→ Documented existing site conditions
→ Began refining ideas for what to build

Site.

Week Two

→ Finalized design solution
→ Finalized program
→ Chose materials
→ Prepared for presentation (drawings and models)

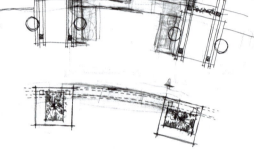

Design sketches (weeks two and three).

"Week two was spent madly discussing, sketching, scribbling, and building models. After much deliberation, the students agreed on a single curved structure along the south edge of the site with covered pavilions at each end and a trellis in the center. A barbecue, mailbox kiosks, additional seating, and a community cherry tree were also planned. Cedar was chosen as the framing material for the pavilions based on contacts with a local cedar distributor. Presentation drawings and a beautiful model were created over the [second] weekend, in preparation for a meeting with the Noji Gardens community on Monday. At the end of the week, all agreed that the group design process was both efficient and satisfying!" [Erin Sonntag and Laurie Stallings]

Week Three

→ Met with community to present design proposals (on first day of week)
→ Revised design based on comments from community members
→ Began site work
→ Laid out foundation
→ Began digging and excavating ("ceremoniously broke ground" with shovels painted with gold spray paint)

Class presentation.

It takes a while to get out of the ground. [Steve]

Week Four

(*Note:* The typical week starts here; students are on site four times a week: Monday, Wednesday, Friday, and Saturday for four hours.)

→ Continued excavation work
→ Cut and shaped reinforcing bars
→ Tied and placed rebar
→ Continued design work (structural analysis and production of working drawings)

Concrete delivery.

Week Five

→ Unloaded, mixed, and poured concrete
→ Laid firebrick for barbecue area
→ Cut and built concrete forms for barbecue and curved column bases

Footings and brickwork (weeks four and five).

Week Six

→ Continued construction of template for curved wall formwork
→ Built wall formwork
→ Placed Simpson brackets and anchor bolts
   (*Note:* Simpson Strong-Tie is a company that manufactures construction connectors and other structural building products.)
→ Completed remaining concrete pours

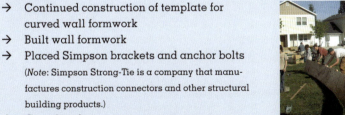

Curved wall formwork.

Week Seven
→ Caught up on odds and ends while waiting for delivery of cedar wood
→ Spread dirt from excavation and recently delivered quarter-minus gravel, which contains pieces that are ¼" or smaller
→ Began work on pavilion with a small load of cedar (picked up by instructor)
→ Raised posts, installed cross bracing, and attached beams and rafters
→ Laid out location of concrete pavers and benches on northeast corner of site

Fun with formwork—concrete paver forms.

Week Eight
→ Fabricated shear panels for pavilion (cut, ground, and welded steel in shop, and then sent components to galvanizer)
→ Erected cedar columns
→ Corrected misplaced column base with flitch plate detail

Cedar posts.

"While the metal shop crew was making sparks fly, the rest of the class erected the first cedar posts. As they did this, they realized that a miscalculation had occurred in the placement of a Simpson Strong-Tie. One of the ties was two inches off and already cast in place. The class came up with the solution of creating a flitch plate from the misplaced tie [to the rest of the structure]. Every design must have one small imperfection!" [Erin Sonntag and Laurie Stallings]

Week Nine

→ Laminated curved beams (Monday and Wednesday)
→ Cut and placed rafters (in the rain, on Friday)
→ Cut, screwed, and trimmed purlins (on a sunny Saturday)
→ Worked with volunteers from local organizations to plant and landscape the site (Saturday)

Week Ten

→ Installed tongue-and-groove cedar decking, building paper, flashing, skip sheathing, and shingles on first roof
→ Installed some shear panels (returned from galvanizer)
→ Added through-bolts to selected connections
→ Continued work on neighborhood kiosks
→ Completed tables and benches
→ Began decking on second roof
→ Trimmed rafter ends and applied paraffin protection
→ Hosted an informal review with University of Washington Professors Frank Ching, Barry Onouye, and Doug Zuberbuhler at the end of the week

Week Eleven

→ Completed second roof
→ Completed neighborhood kiosks
→ Installed remaining shear panels and tables and benches
→ Completed mosaic designs
→ Spread woodchips over areas of dirt
→ Spread a final load of gravel underneath pavilions
→ Assisted electrician with wiring from solar panels to the pavilion
→ Cleaned the site

Opening Day: ribbon-cutting ceremony and community barbecue

Party and ribbon cutting

Finished detail

FINISHING
TOPPING OUT

When a project reaches its highest elevation and nears completion, John and his students practice the tradition of topping out—placing a small tree, a branch, or greenery at the structure's highest point. **Fig. 21** He then marks the end of the course with a class photo on the Thursday afternoon before Friday's graduation. **Fig. 22** Students climb ladders, wield hammers, lean out windows, and wave from roofs. Some are even putting the finishing touches on the project. The following day at the graduation ceremony, John presents each student with a gift—a signed piece of wood that the instructors have made as a memento of the course. Students soon figure out the mysterious gift is part of a puzzle that spells out "Home Design/Build," the course's date, and Yestermorrow's logo. **Fig. 23** What was an "inscrutable chunk of wood" becomes, as John says, "a symbol of team effort. It shows the collaborative nature of their class project and allows them to take a bit of the project home with them."

Fig. 21 Topping out with greenery on the roof framing of John's Yestermorrow Home Design/Build Studio project, 2006.

Fig. 22 John's class photo for picnic table storage shed project, Yestermorrow Home Design/Build studio, 2007.

Fig. 23 Class puzzle at graduation, Yestermorrow Home Design/Build studio, 2014.

T-SHIRT DESIGN

T-shirts are design/build swag that further brings the group together. Over the years, Jersey Devil's members made T-shirts related to their projects, and now they ask students to design each studio's shirt. In Steve's class, although the group as a whole still decides the winner, this process is the only time students compete, suggesting that, with the exception of this special event, design work proceeds by building consensus rather than winning proposals. Jim mentions the T-shirts during the first week of studio so that students can begin formulating ideas. Once the studio has come up with a scheme and building has started, the T-shirt design offers a return to the schematic design process with the images and ideas from the project. In 2015, the University of Washington design/build studio incorporated the project's cross section into its T-shirt design, and the graphic design for Jim's 2014 studio included a saw blade imprinted with the elevation of the Coffee Kiosk. Since many institutions have a student art center with silk-screening equipment, it is also possible to "build" your own T-shirts. **Figs. 24–25**

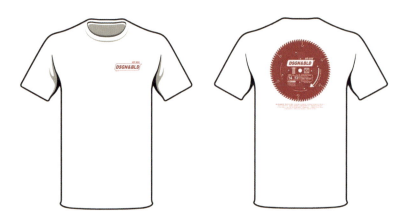

Fig. 24 T-shirt design for University of Miami's 2014 design/build studio.

Fig. 25 Students wearing T-shirts designed for Steve's 2011 studio.

RIBBON CUTTING

When the last nail is set, the final carriage bolts are tightened, and the topcoat of sealant has dried, it's time to celebrate. Steve closes out projects with a ribbon-cutting, one final group clap, and oftentimes a celebratory meal. **Fig. 26** After completing the Helping Link project in 2010, students joined their clients for a Vietnamese meal and a cake inscribed with congratulations. At the dedication of the waiting shelter in 2006, members of the Mt. Baker Housing Association prepared food for the studio after the ribbon-cutting ceremony and speeches. To finish out the New Face Project at Danny Woo in 2003, gardeners brought meals they prepared from their harvest, and each student had a chance to spread seeds in the new plant beds. For Jim's Orchid Pavilion project, everyone gathered around a bonfire to make "goofy" speeches. To conclude the Mobile PermaKitchen project, the client cooked a meal in the courtyard of the University of Miami's architecture school. And for Yestermorrow's Public Interest Design/Build, Steve says that "graduation ceremonies are held around the fire at Dave Sellers's Temple of Dindur (a play on the Egyptian Temple of Dendur) in Warren, featuring graduation speeches, diplomas singed in the fire, adult beverages, and Indian leg wrestling." I am told that Jim is unbeaten in these matches.

Fig. 26 Ribbon cutting for the Garden Gathering Place at Danny Woo Community Garden, 2007.

ACKNOWLEDGMENT

Fundraising yields the reciprocal instrument of acknowledgment. Thank-you notes and credits in print and on websites are a necessity to finalize the important relationship between donor and project. Contributors will also appreciate publicity that can be generated from their involvement in the project. For the finished project, Steve installs a plaque, which is typically donated by an etching company also included on the list of donors. **Fig. 27** Contributors receive a copy of the publication that documents the project and includes the full list of those who helped out. Donations that go through universities often qualify for gifts and privileges. With Steve's projects, the University of Washington invites those who contribute more than $1,000 to special events. Invitations to ribbon-cutting ceremonies, finishing parties, and celebratory meals also serve as ways to acknowledge donors and volunteers.

PUBLICATION

Jim and Steve both ask their design/build studios to produce a booklet that documents the project. Ideally, students work on this during the studio's term, because after classes finish, it can be hard to find time and to coordinate completion. Making the book provides a forum for additional collaboration and affords opportunities to reflect on design/build—both as it continues and after it is completed. Such books not only document but also continue a process of analysis, speculation, and learning. For students, they serve as a richly crafted record of community interaction and accomplishments. For instructors, the book is an active tool for considering subsequent projects, an archive for the institution, a resource to show potential clients and prospective donors, and a document that can be shared with colleagues to open discussions about design/build pedagogy and its deeply drawn process.

Fig. 27 Plaque acknowledging donors and participants in the Wellspring design/build project, 2009.

Fig. 28 Cover and title page of student publication for Beacon Food Forest project, 2013.

LESSONS

Design/build intertwines the way you learn with what you learn. Its setting combines studio, workshop, laboratory, and jobsite, and the things you make there are constantly talking back to you at full scale, in real time, and alongside the shared experience of others. One of design/build's many lessons is that building is a process of learning. This process has its footings in edification, in the way that it builds character as well as constructs buildings. Design/build teaches us how to make edifices, even if they are modest, while it also teaches us about ourselves by revealing what an ethics of design and construction means to us; and it has the potential to combine practical instruction with modes of practice—not just in the design profession but also more broadly in life.

EXPERIENCE

At the core of design/build's lessons is, quite simply, experience. Steve invokes the hammer as an instrument of experience: "Nothing can tell you more about a hammer than a blood blister when you hit your thumb. The words *blood blister* don't mean anything until you've smashed it."

Sometimes the design/build experience is extraordinary—working in a foreign country or helping cut the ribbon for a nonprofit's community center expansion. **Figs. 01-02** Jim recalls that, during the Mexico projects, students were quite literally learning from the masters—the construction "maestros" who collaborated with the design/build studio and taught them how to lay bricks. Other times, experience can be as seemingly mundane as digging and pouring. But we learn from each aspect of construction along the way. In designing and building, we find the extraordinary in the ordinary. Materials, context, and collaborators all come together to make up this experience. With design/build, you don't just plan for it, or think and talk about it. You do it.

Fig. 01 Solar Kitchen, San Lucas, Mexico, University of Washington Mexico Design/Build, 2004.

Fig. 02 Testing the Scheffler Reflector for the Solar Kitchen.

SKILL

Students of design/build gain skills in building and in linking design conception with construction. Steve summarizes this outcome, adding the equally crucial skill of collaboration: "They're hopefully going to learn a little about how to build and how to work in a team, which is basically the way most things are done in the architecture and construction world. Very few things are actually created by one person." This range of proficiency—from individual to group—is one of the primary lessons of design/build. **Fig. 03**

Fig. 03 Welding for the Lao Highland project, Seattle, 2008.

Skills gained depend on a project's context, materials, and building systems. But even a partial list points toward a diverse skill set that extends from operations to organization: cutting, welding, drilling and fastening, reading and culling wood, laying out a site, managing and estimating materials, talking with clients, and scheduling and dividing work. Students also assemble a repertoire for joining materials: if welding, then fillets, grooves, and spots; if woodworking, then toe-nails, face-nails, bolts, and screws. Like the joints they make, such skills travel well. I tell my students the story of Japanese carpenters who bear mental catalogs of joints as they move from project to project.

Skills readily link to what are often called the "practical" lessons of design/build. Repeating and practicing operations such as cutting, drilling, and fastening raises students' skill levels and prepares them to work with constraints as well as improvise with unexpected conditions. Did you know that a circular saw can cut curves if their radii are large enough? Steve says he's heard others joke that's why it's called a "circular" saw. How do you clean up a splintered end cut? A wood file pulled along the corner chamfers—more precisely, "eases"—the edges and can even visually "straighten" a slightly out-of-square cut. Is the board splitting when you nail near its end? You can blunt the nail's end with a strike of the hammer. Skills built upon skills, fastened by experience.

SELF-RELIANCE

Building builds confidence. Making a successful saw cut—the blade screaming and sawdust spraying—not only is satisfying but also can be liberating. Raising a beam and bolting it in place is exhilarating. According to Jim, design/build "gives students confidence in themselves, so they're willing to take something on."

Fig. 04 Load testing a plywood construction in Steve's 2008 design/build studio.

The task of building provides a safe and rigorous context for speculation. When we learn to use tools and assemble building components, we understand where and how hazards occur. The veil of the construction site is lifted and fears are mitigated. This surety extends back into the design process as well. Jim continues, "Sometimes if you don't have the experience of the build part of it, you really can't take risks, because you're not connected to what you're designing." Design/build is not just a class or a mode of project delivery—it is an attitude. **Fig. 04** The studio offers lessons not as conceit but in boldness.

Materials themselves also build confidence. To know the weight of tubular steel, to have lifted a bag of concrete, or to hold the memory of a 6x6's girth is to haul building into the realm of design.

RESILIENCE

Design/build also teaches resilience. Jim and Rocco were working with the Parks Division and had previously met with a homeowner who resisted the project. Halfway through the semester, the project came to a halt, and Jim, along with his students, had to find a new project. Their fast-track design process was a function of lessons learned from earlier in the semester, when they spent weeks refining the pavilion design that ultimately would not be built. They also borrowed—and even perfected—material systems from the previous project.

> **I say that my students have attitude. They feel more comfortable on a jobsite later when they're architects. And they're also not afraid to make decisions and to make things.** [Steve]

On Monday, May 19, in the eighth week of the quarter, Seattle Tilth, the client for Steve's 2008 studio, requested that all construction be stopped. The city's parks department wanted to review additional construction documents, which the class immediately submitted to the department's engineer. But negotiations continued, and the client asked the studio to deliver the frame and the prefabricated trusses to be erected by volunteers after a resolution (but also after the studio's term was over). With little time remaining, the class found this scenario unacceptable. Since Seattle Tilth had not yet paid for the materials, the studio looked for another site. The students' resolve yielded a new client—the Lao Highlands Association, but a week of adapting the pre-fabricated building components to the new site's constraints left less than a week for construction. Rain fell and final exams began, but the members of the studio persisted—discovering, along the way, that they could save time by building the community pavilion from the top down. Concrete was curing in Sonotubes, columns were plumbed, and cross bracing was fastened as the last roofing panel was set on Wednesday evening, just in time and ready for Thursday's party.

TEAMWORK

Learning to work as a team and to collaborate, sometimes in the face of sheer labor, is a design/build lesson that complements experience and self-reliance. In the preparations to move the modules for the Motes Orchid Pavilion, Jim's students referred to the loading process as "collaborative pushing and pulling." [see "Shop" in "Toolbox"] For Yestermorrow's 2005 Community Design/Build project, the isolated location of the Mad River Path Trail Shelter meant that students had to work together as they carried the building components along the hiking trail. **Figs. 05-07**

Fig. 05 Carrying "bents" to the site of the Mad River Path Trail Shelter, Warren, Vermont, 2005.

Fig. 06 Components laid out at the trail shelter site.

Fig. 07 Completed trail shelter.

TOLERANCE

Crafting a project does not always mean perfect joints, just as it also does not necessarily bring forth ideal partnerships. There is always some play. Building needs those margins of error, and collaborating requires patience. Construction's dictionary is full of terms with dual meanings. Tolerance refers to one way people and things address difference. It allows for leeway, which then sustains the connections that are being made—whether between collaborators or joined materials. The ways we relate to others require flexibility, just as construction joints must allow materials to move, expand, and change. Group work can be messy, but another's viewpoint is a matter not just for consideration but also often for innovation.

In working with material systems, design/build teaches us when to be precise. In working with others, it teaches us how to negotiate. The former can be quantified: we try for 1/16" tolerance, which is the allowable amount of variation in any measurement. The latter is more qualitative but quantifiable in its outcome: we work toward consensus. Students will also learn that these tolerances—both materially and socially—vary with scale and location. A detail might require a more precise connection when a small error can be systematically increased with repetition throughout the whole. But, in other contexts, a joint created too tightly will not allow materials to expand and contract. And with group work, sticking too closely to an opinion about a specific part might obscure the vision of an entire project. John tells a story of a student who made violins for a living:

"We had broken up into groups on the first day, and each group of students was cutting scrap wood so they could practice their circular saw skills and so we could evaluate how each student handled the tool. In one of the groups was a student who was a professional violin maker. After all the other groups had finished their cuts, that group was still talking about the process. I went over to see what the holdup was and found them using a very small, extremely precise ruler (that could measure hundredths of an inch) to lay out the measurement. Based on the violin maker's experience, they were looking to make a cut in framing lumber to a luthier's tolerances using a violin maker's tool. I called the whole class together and said, 'We need to talk about tolerance.' It was a great lesson for me and for the whole class. I use the story each year to explain what the tolerances are for our cutting." [*Note*: A luthier repairs musical string instruments.]

IMPLICATIONS

While designing, we might not fully consider how it will be built. While building, we are asked to reconsider how it was designed. Lines trace accountability, and Steve reminds us that design implications are not just visualized but also experienced. You cannot hide in design/build. The effects of decisions through every stage of the process are readily visible in what is actually being made. Small differences generally carry great significance for built work, and

Hopefully, students learn the implications of the lines they draw on a piece of paper. [Steve]

this is especially true for design/build's often intimate scales. By renovating a small living space, my students came to understand a partition wall's placement in terms of inches on the site, rather than in modules of feet measured and debated in studio. On site, they understood the implications for how the space would be used. This is a level of engagement with details and human occupation that students have likely not experienced in previous studios.

Materials make us humble. In his studios, John makes clear the case that designers must understand what materials can do and their potential to be active agents in our design process, correlating directly and precisely with building. It can be difficult to actualize what you draw because, as Steve notes, "Building materials and assemblies are not going to be the way you represent them on the computer." Those lines become material, which then—for students pursuing professional work—denote precise specifications grounded in how buildings go together. **Figs. 08–10** Steve adds site design and layout to this connection between design/build education and professional work:

"As an architect, you don't have to build all your own buildings, but you should be able to go to the site and lay it out. You need to learn how to put a building on the site. We learn about batter boards, we learn about the builder's level, and we learn how to take a drawing and put it on a piece of land." [Steve]

Fig. 08 Structural bent for the Mad River Path Trail Shelter in the Yestermorrow shop, 2005.

Fig. 09 Truss layout for Lao Highlands project, 2008.

Fig. 10 Gathering Place at Danny Woo Community Garden, 2007.

POLITICS

Design/build also has political implications. It can transform the relations between people, as it also reshapes our links to the things and environments around us.

When Steve makes the connection between teaching and practicing design/build, he doesn't politicize education, but instead makes the more significant case for education's role in the *polis*—the broader community linked by place and the daily activities that make that place work:

"Take a look at the guys you're talking to—they're all products of the 1960s, and those '60s values are totally responsible for where we all ended up. In the '60s, the ecology movement was prominent, which translated into energy-efficient buildings, and now it is public-interest design that offers change. If you can find somebody to pay for it, you can do something that needs to get built for somebody who can't afford to pay for it. How can you lose if you get all the students working on a project for a nonprofit? As an educator, that's a big part of my agenda."

Politics also mean that names change—*ecology, sustainability, public interest*—but firmly held goals remain stable. For Jersey Devil and with design/build, there is a consistent objective—"a political philosophy" that, Steve likes to say, is sometimes a "hidden agenda," but in reality and particularly with public projects is "not really that hidden."

> **Politics are part of architecture, and one goal of the design/build program is to allow the students to see that architecture can really make a huge difference in the lives of people who can't afford it.** [Steve]

COMMUNITY

Design/build connects participants to community. **Figs. 11–12** Steve lays out the social implications and responsibilities this work prompts:

"Hopefully [students will] become a different type of architect because they've worked in the studio's nonprofit context. They'll see that working for people where architecture really makes a difference in their lives can be a potential career changer. Maybe instead of working at the top of the food chain like most in the profession, they will become more community-minded architects and have a richer career because they'll have those social values, they'll know how to build, they'll know the realities and the responsibilities of building, and they'll be able to work effectively on the team with a lot of different kinds of people. That's the goal."

Learning how to build links with how to collaborate and asks us to consider a project's value, what it means for the community, and how other work might follow a responsible course. Teaching design/build has coincided with Jersey Devil's growing interest in public projects.

"We're always looking for community service projects, and Jersey Devil has moved from doing houses for people with a certain amount of means to doing these little community projects with students. It's an interesting development, where all of us have gone." [Steve]

Fig. 11 Ribbon cutting for Farmer's Market Bandstand, Warren, Vermont, 1994.

Fig. 12 Concert at Farmer's Market Bandstand.

GOOD LIFE

The lessons of design/build occur in an immediate context that includes the thing being built, its site, and the client and community. These studios have the potential to connect design with everyday life, but design/build is also magically real. **Fig. 13** In his teaching process, John invokes the magic made possible by a designer's knowledge of how to realize projects:

"I tell them on the first morning that we're involved in a process that's literally magic. We start out with nothing, and we end up with something. If I told you I was going to pull a rabbit out of an empty hat, you would call it magic. Well, that's what we're going to do. So the project is the manifestation of that magical process, and they're part of it—they are committed to it."

Fig. 13 Class photo for John's Home Design/Build project for the East Warren Schoolhouse porch, 2000.

And it really is magic. Design/build is not just a way of learning, but also a way of living. Jersey Devil has made a practice of having fun and living a life immersed in making. **Fig. 14** When Steve says, "students see that these are some guys who have a lot of laugh lines and have had pretty good lives—I mean, you can't wipe that smile off Jim's face," he crafts a rich fusion of Jim's and John's perspectives:

"The fact that you can do it—and the magic that John is talking about—is really a huge lesson that it is all really possible. And that's a life lesson that applies to a lot more than just making things."

REFLECTIVE BUILDING

Design/build's lessons also join the practical with the pedagogical. Too often, the former is isolated as rationale for design/build coursework. Students and faculty alike cite design/build for its "practical experience"—there is no question that students learn skills, a tangible outcome of the process. Practically

Fig. 14 Ribbon cutting celebration for Wheeler Brook Apartments Picnic Pavilion, Warren, Vermont, Yestermorrow Public Interest Design/Build, 2009.

Fig. 15 Construction of Deane Nature Preserve Pedestrian Bridge at Yestermorrow, 2011.

Fig. 16 Deane Nature Preserve Pedestrian Bridge, Poultney, Vermont.

speaking, design/build may also bridge with professional work, handshaking with postgraduate life. An off-campus context and work with "real" clients is not unlike an architectural internship. But in another sense, design/build is the most impractical of teaching methods. It extends already-expanded contact hours from the studio to a jobsite, it requires consistent balance between design aspirations and logistical constraint, and its budgetary limitations require massive outputs of unskilled, volunteer labor. **Figs. 15–16**

So why do we do it? Design/build offers time to practice: it makes room for experimentation, which is integral to learning by doing; and this practice allows time for experience: for understanding a site, working in groups, handling materials, and listening to clients. Pedagogically, design/build returns students to the basics—elemental concepts and techniques first explored in early design studios. By extension, this context offers students a place of reflection. Students often note that the atmosphere of the studio—perhaps amplified by its plein air context—quite literally opens things up for reflection. The studio offers the time and place for students to consider their educational experiences. It looks backward and forward. Design/build studios connect to possible futures in design and construction professions, while also delving deeply into the foundations of architectural education. And although it may not constitute a capstone course in the traditional sense of a holistic product, the design/build studio does offer a holistic process that gathers thinking, making, and collaborating. **Fig. 17**

Fig. 17 John as the "Rebar Yogi" on the site of the Snail House, 1972.

CASES

RURAL KITCHEN

Year: 2010

Studio: MIT Design/Build Cambodia

Instructors: Jim Adamson, John Ochsendorf

Organizers: Ethan Lacy, Zach Lamb

Students: Tiffany Chu, Sam Cohen, Lee Dykxhoorn, Adam Galletly, Julie Gawendo, Rebecca Gould, Alorah Harman, Lisa Hedstrom, Sian Kleindienst, Andrea Love, Joseph Nunez, Lisa Pauli, Pamela Ritchot, Sian Siobhan Rockcastle, Julianna Sassaman, Yan-Ping Wang

Client: Ampil Peam School

Location: Siem Reap Province, Cambodia

Size: 300 square feet (covered), 600 square feet (landscape)

Donors: Jay Pritzker Academy, MIT Public Service Center, MIT Department of Architecture

Budget: approximately $6,000

Duration: 19 days (30 days including preplanning and project wrap-up)

1
View of Rural Kitchen.

2
Rural Kitchen during breakfast.

For the Rural Kitchen project, Jim traveled to Siem Reap Province a week in advance and worked with Ethan Lacy on project preplanning. They met with the Pritzker Academy, investigated the resources in local villages, studied local building traditions, and discovered recent applications of precast columns and footings, as well as an older vernacular of arched vaults that would inform the project. This preparation facilitated the fast-tracking of the project so that designing and building would occur during MIT's winter intersession. Zach Lamb remained at the site after the studio's allotted time to help Jim with wrap-up and documentation.

Fourteen architecture students, three civil engineering students, and one landscape architecture student designed and built the project. Students moved between the design/build project and MIT's design charrettes for expanding the Priztker Academy campus, so at any given time there were five or six members of the team on site.

The project's design phase lasted three days. Students arrived in the evening on Monday, January 4, and the next morning visited the Pritzker Academy campus. After touring three possible sites, they decided to design and build a kitchen and cafeteria for the Ampil Peam community's government-run school, which hosts sixty students in four classrooms without electricity. Students based the project choice on where they saw the greatest need.

The following day, students consulted the school's director and cook about the kitchen layout, and Jim supervised site analysis and measurement. On the third day, design of the cafeteria and kitchen continued with two primary schemes. Students considered one arrangement surrounding the well, but chose to pursue a more linear plan that engaged but did not encircle the water source, which would have a limited lifespan.

During the design process and even into the construction phase, students used fundamental tools of visualization and representation. Jim notes: "It was all sketched. This was so fast-track that we didn't even build physical models for this one, though we did have schematic CAD drawings for layout. In the tradition of Jersey Devil, the fine details were worked out on site."

This type of design communication also lent itself to social communication, particularly with Pong, the local welder and foreman: "These details would be drawn on the ground, right there in the dirt." The team broke ground on January 8, and site work involved excavation for eight precast columns and compaction of delivered dirt. With this latter process, students improvised with materials available on site to create tools known as "elephants' feet"—tree stumps with bamboo handles. According to one student, "tamping became the song of the afternoon." A local resident saw the hard work and brought in his homemade ride-on compactor to help with the process. While this site work was taking place, another group of students inventoried available building materials—from steel to cisterns—at the local hardware stores.

The next day, the slab was poured and columns were set. Jim recalls that the construction system was "like building a table upside down," forming a very rigid connection between precast column and slab by drilling through the column bases to insert rebar that carries loads to the concrete base. Prior to pouring the slab, students researched alternatives to traditional concrete mixtures and discovered that they could replace 20 to 30 percent of the cement with ash that came from burning rice husks as fuel to heat local brick kilns. This combination of design and research was rewarding for the students:

"Gratification followed when a contractor arrived unannounced at our site via motorcycle this afternoon, saying that he had to see it with his own eyes to believe it. He left laughing, impressed." [Alorah Harman]

At the same time, students mocked up options for the vaulting system that would house the kitchen's secure food storage area. A group of students worked with Jim and MIT professor John Ochsendorf first to study systems built without formwork and then to consider how the use of formwork for brick arches could expedite the process. They explored corbel vaults similar to those in Cambodia's temples and tested the reduced thrust of catenary arches. Students also experimented with rammed earth walls and earth bricks, mixing soil with concrete in premade forms. And at the end of the fourth day, Ethan Lacy marveled at the project's intensive labor and pace:

"Today some serious progress on the brickwork for the kitchen. Here we are enjoying the relative cool of the late afternoon sun after a long day of laying bricks. Some local guys are building the oven for the cook stove, and the brick walls on the right are to support the serving counter. It's day four of building, and we're already on a slab building walls, with columns in place, and two of the four trusses have been fabricated (by a local welder). I've never seen a project move this quickly."

In the workdays that followed, truss fabrication proceeded with local steel and collaboration with a welder from the village. The school's students climbed onto mock-ups of the trusses to help test their strength before they were raised into place. The design/build team continued with masonry work, buttering and laying bricks and constructing the stove and vaults. The rainwater catchment system spawned an activity the students called "cistern wrestling." To place three precast concrete cisterns, they used brute force as well as a more finessed method described by Tiffany Chu as a "bamboo roller, skid, and lever system to muscle them into place."

Being in a foreign place with a limited time frame required improvisation. Fence posts became landscape planters and also served as formwork for the slab (where they remained in place) and for rammed-earth bases of the bench seating. Foil lining from hotels' air-conditioning systems served as material for the radiant barriers that captured the radiated heat below the roof in an air space, which could be purged with vents. Students also adapted local building methods: bamboo columns, rather than conventional shores, supported formwork for the cast concrete bench tops.

"The Rural Kitchen project was an educational experience for all. We were greatly influenced by the rich heritage of local construction, and our sustainable sensibilities allowed us to adopt and adapt these traditions. Just about every village has cottage industries where concrete is used to produce precast column assemblies, fence posts, pavers, and cistern tanks, and we incorporated them all. Locally fired brick was also readily available. With the help of local masons, we used it to construct the energy-efficient two-pot stove, the counter supports, and the vaulted granary." [Jim]

Throughout the project, students developed ties with the community and its cultural context. They had corresponded with Cambodian children during the fall semester, and on the fifth day of the project they met with these pen pals to have lunch, play chess, and exchange gifts, and on the following day, they explored the cultural sites of Angkor Wat. Local schoolchildren were active participants in the project. Student Alorah Harman remarked, "As always, the site was bustling with children: climbing into our wheelbarrows, swarming the well, yelling, playing, laughing, and lining up as an impromptu audience to scrutinize our every endeavor."

With just a few workdays remaining, a reduced crew followed a long punch list, and the community began to occupy the project. On January 22, Zach Lamb summarized the jobsite's new rhythms, its final stages, and the joy of both work and play:

"The crew is down to four. After sending off three more of our team this evening, the crazy energy of the full jobsite has subsided a bit. Our much smaller group is settling into a new pace for the final stretch: slower, quieter, but kind of nice in its own right.

The landscape pavers are nearly done. Plumbing for the cisterns is well on its way. The vault is eagerly awaiting its liberation from the formwork. The last countertop has been poured. The radiant barrier has been delivered, but we are still waiting on the metal team to return to do the ceiling installation.

We are really closing in on the end. The project looks and feels great. Every day we are surprised and delighted to see how the school and village are taking to the structure…a few teachers taking a break on the rammed-earth benches, a late-afternoon conversation on the bamboo planters, a group of kids delighting in hopscotch-like fun on the grid of pavers. It is going to be a well-used and well-loved space.

More tomorrow."

Two days later the team removed the formwork for the vaults, painted the roof, and sanded the countertop. Students tested the cistern and completed installing the first flush system that purges the first—and often contaminated—runoff from the roof. And then on January 25, they joined schoolkids for an early-morning celebratory breakfast.

"Before flying out Monday night, we planned to have breakfast with the schoolkids during their normal 6 AM mealtime. We were particularly excited to see the structure put to its designed use...How would the cook use the spaces in the kitchen? Would the kids follow the circulation paths that we imagined? Would the space be big enough to accommodate the whole school at once?

All in all, the structure seemed to perform really well. The kitchen seemed to be intuitive and convenient to use. The stove drew well with only minimal smoke in the space. After some prodding from Steve [McCambridge], the kids did follow the progression from washing up at the pump to the serving counter to the eating areas.

A few surprises: the planters with bamboo became an impromptu volleyball court; the kids managed to fit twelve to fifteen people on each of the little rammed-earth benches; after the kids ate, there was first a puppy and then several chickens that made their way through the site making their breakfast off of any spilled bits of rice.

Our estimates of 'kids per linear meter' of bench were far, far exceeded. Nearly the entire school was able to find a spot to sit to eat on the rammed-earth benches (nearly exclusively boys) or the planter boxes out front (nearly all girls). Though we did not have time to design or prototype the movable furniture for the project, it seems safe to say that the kids will make the most of the available areas." [Zach]

When Zach described this final event, he began to see how the group's design/build work was going to be used, already understanding the implications of selected materials, rendered volumes, and drawn lines.

3–4

Full-scale studies of masonry arches helped Jim's studio group determine the most efficient roof system for Siem Reap's kitchen. After a series of explorations without formwork, students determined that bricks laid on forms provided the most direct technology for their budget and schedule.

5

Site preparation.

6

Laying up bricks.

7

Testing mixes with fly ash.

8

Local supply of steel.

9

Jim recalls how Ethan Lacy created a three-dimensional computer model "to the delight of the young children."

10

Exploring cultural sites.

11

Laying fence posts as forms for the concrete slab.

12

On-site fabrication of steel trusses.

13

Children help test loads on steel trusses.

14
Installation of steel roof trusses.

15
Detail of rain collection system.

16
Bamboo posts supporting
bench formwork.

17
Moving cistern pipes into place.

19

18
Food preparation area.

19
Dining area and court.

20–21, 24
Meal to celebrate project's completion.

22
Kitchen area.

23
Design/build studio students
and instructors.

24

1

URBAN FARM SUPERSHED

Year: 2012

Studio: Neighborhood Design/Build Studio, College of Built Environments, University of Washington

Instructors: Steve Badanes, Jake LaBarre

Students: Giselle Altea, Emily Aune, Jordan Bell, Jessica Fabro, Wendy Fan, Louisa Galassini, Tera Hatfield, Kelly Hogg, Kevin Lang, Carolyn LeCompte, Erin McDade, David Neuville, Arnulfo Ramirez, Jason Sawyer, Tyrel Sullivan, Joseph Wessinger, Christopher Yee

Teaching Assistant: Ji Shon

Clients: University of Washington Farm, Seattle Youth Garden Works, and Hardy Plant Society of Seattle

Location: Center for Urban Horticulture at University of Washington Botanic Gardens, Seattle, Washington

Size: 462 square feet (covered), 297 square feet (enclosed)

Donors: Howard S. Wright Endowment, Roloson Foundation, JAS Design Build, University of Washington Farm, Seattle Youth Gardenworks, Center for Urban Horticulture, Hardy Plant Society of Washington, Stewart Lumber, Bluestar Electric, Nucor Steel, Jeff Moore / Montana Originals, Rae Louise Moore, Mountain High Gardening / Erin Lau, Bragdon Shields, Damon Smith, Dave Lipe / 16d Design/Build, College of Built Environments Dean's Office, Restore

Budget: $11,000

Project duration: 11 weeks (spring quarter at University of Washington)

Class time: Monday, Wednesday, Friday from 12:30 pm to 5:30 pm, and Saturday from 10 am to 2 pm

An interdisciplinary group of seventeen students worked on the Supershed project: eleven architecture students, two landscape architecture students, two dual-degree students studying both architecture and real estate, one architecture and construction management dual major, and one student in the construction management graduate program. The construction process included both site-built and prefabricated components. Students chose a site at the intersection of a walking path and an access road, along the northern edge of Union Bay Natural Area.

"The Supershed differed from typical NDBS projects because the site is enormous and isolated from the urban context. It's located in the Union Bay Natural Area, a 74-acre public wildlife preserve on Lake Washington. Originally a peat wetland, the area was a landfill from 1926 through the mid-1960s. Today, thanks to ongoing wetland restoration, the space is dedicated to recreation, research, and education programs." [Steve]

The studio developed the "supershed" concept to house multiple programs. The project's three clients asked for three different storage areas, a solar greenhouse for plant starts, a covered outdoor classroom with built-in seating, covered bike storage, and two tool-washing stations linked to a rainwater collection system.

"The roof form emerged as we organized the program and thought about desired solar exposure. The class recognized that the outdoor classroom should face the field, the greenhouse could store heat with the water-filled barrels adjacent to the windows, and the tool storage could open toward the parking area." [Jake LaBarre]

The shed roof unified these diverse spaces with a diagonal ridge as well as the combination of customized trusses and sloping top plates. This double-pitch roof lifts up to the east and creates an open connection between classroom and farm, and pitches down to the west for maximum solar exposure over the greenhouse. The inventive roof system sends water in equal amounts to opposite corners of either end, where rain barrels capture the runoff for tool washing.

During the first and second weeks, students generated consensus on a design scheme, which they presented to the clients at the beginning of week three. After continued design development, construction drawings were prepared to convey the project's ideas, its organization, and selected details.

"The construction drawings were developed to the level of basic building layout, wall sections, and a few structural details, similar to typical small building permit level drawings. The building size and spaces were determined, but the details remained diagrammatic. As we moved into construction, students were encouraged to keep drawing, but often with full-scale sketches on plywood or scraps of blocking. Details were then resolved in the form of mock-ups and trial and error." [Jake]

Site work began on the Saturday of week three. Students built the concrete formwork with salvaged wood, which was later repurposed. To reduce costs, quarter-minus crushed gravel provided stable compaction with its ¼" (or smaller) pieces and served as an alternative to concrete slabs.

In the shop, prefabrication included eighteen trusses (with nine different configurations) and twenty wall panels (with three different patterns). The walls' 2x4 frame supported cement board sheathing.

"Some of the students each year have building backgrounds, so a few are usually familiar with production work, but few understand the value of being able to repeatedly build the same size module. When they were making the drawings, we discussed this a bit, as well as the importance of understanding where to leave some room for adjustment. The 'aha' moment started when they stacked all the pieces that were supposed to be exactly the same size in a pile, and it was driven home when we put the tape measure on the assembled building. Also, with the repetitive cuts, they were able to understand more clearly how to get the most out of each piece of wood.

Prefabrication work is a great way to broaden the effectiveness of the studio as a learning environment for all of the students. Often some students do not excel right away at site work (digging/layout/rough construction), because they are still becoming familiar with tools and the physical nature of construction. Their confidence is not yet fully developed, and learning how to build precise elements in a controlled environment allows them an early victory. As they begin to build momentum we work to encourage best practices of craft, problem solving, appropriate solutions, and safety. Also, a well-thought-out process has more room for creative thought throughout. The repetitive nature of the wall structures allowed the typical framing complexities to be somewhat regularized and gave the class a little more room to be creative on the roof form." [Jake]

In the sixth week, prefabricated trusses and wall panels were delivered to the site. Students bolted the wall panels into place on the concrete foundation and fastened trusses with steel hurricane ties.

In weeks seven through nine, students added 2-inch-diameter pressure-treated fence posts and an outer layer of galvanized 4-inch steel mesh to the walls. They then filled the 2-inch nominal space with vegetative material from the farm and wove twigs and branches into mesh. The outdoor classroom walls were slatted with locally milled cedar. Students used leftover formwork boards to make sliding doors. Other details—like the window wall in the greenhouse, rain chain, roof corners, and ridge cap—were completed.

A dedication party and ribbon-cutting ceremony commemorated the project, along with a delivery of wheelbarrows filled with fresh greens from the farm.

"Building on campus is usually a bad idea since the level of bureaucracy and 'turf wars' are even higher than at the city level. However, the site is in the UW Botanic Gardens, far from campus and university life. The immediate site had a university compost facility, where we found most of the vegetative material for the walls. When I went to check out the site, it occurred to me that aside from service vehicles, there was no traffic at the site and we could build a larger structure than is normally permitted by code, something that would be more in scale with the site than a collection of sheds. The tight budget also favored a single simple structure. The project is a great example of the scale and quality of work students can accomplish in a short time frame and with limited resources, if you give them the opportunity." [Steve]

The project's open structure, its walls with vegetative material, and its clear logic of building—the clerestory becomes a chord truss over the classroom opening—all support the Urban Farm's goals to demonstrate urban farming's potential and to teach the impact of food choices. An active background for farming, the shed joins in the process of education. The way the building was made also speaks to the farm's emphasis on participatory education.

1 (p.137)
View of Supershed from southwest.

2
Drawing of truss layout.

3
Truss layout and jig.

4
Typical truss for Supershed roof.

5
Bundled trusses ready for delivery.

6
Construction documents.

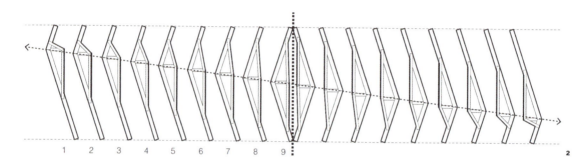

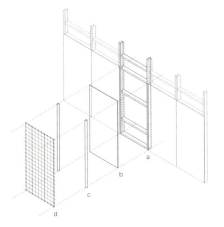

9

7
Installing trusses at Supershed
site.

8
Installing wall panels.

9
Drawing of wall panel system.

10
Weaving the twig wall.

11
Twig wall (detail).

12 (overleaf)
North elevation of completed
Supershed.

13

14

15

13
North elevation under
construction.

14
Urban farm and Supershed under
construction.

15
Ribbon-cutting ceremony.

16
View from outdoor classroom toward farm.

17
Detail of outdoor classroom seating.

18
Storage room.

HOME DESIGN/BUILD OUTBUILDINGS

Year: Ongoing since 1990

Studio: Home Design/Build course, Yestermorrow Design/ Build School, Waitsfield, Vermont

Instructors: John Ringel and Kathy Meyer (along with additional instructors)

Location: Central and northern Vermont

Size: Varies (approximately 100 square feet)

Budget: Varies (typically $2,400 for garden sheds)

Project duration: 9 afternoons (total of 36 hours)

Class time: Design sessions (8 am to noon and 7 pm to 10 pm); build sessions (1 pm to 5 pm)

1
Project with chicken run addition.

"From high school students to retirees"—Jim's summary of the diverse group that John teaches in his Yestermorrow class highlights the wide appeal and everyday relevance of design/build. Realtors, contractors, architects, engineers, teenagers, CEOs, DIYers, and even a violin maker have all taken the Home Design/Build course. And they come from many places, including Texas, Florida, Wisconsin, New York, and New England, and from as far away as Alaska, Hawaii, and the Caribbean. John's typical student has little or no experience in design and construction. A few in each class have some familiarity with hand tools, one or two students will be considering design/build as a career, and "occasionally we have a professional builder who wants to figure out how designers/architects think." Graduates of architecture programs have also enrolled in the course for the building experience. John acknowledges the challenges of this diversity, but this "amalgam of unique people, places, and programs" enhances the educational experience for teacher and student alike. This variety of backgrounds also means that John must start from the same point: he begins with the assumption that everyone knows nothing. It is a back-to-basics approach.

And yet John's course schedule has the complexity of a train timetable. It is a matrix of parallel tracks that are organized around main sessions of design and build, move in multiple directions, and enlist an array of teaching modes with crossings of house tours, technical talks, guest lectures, and pinup reviews. Each day includes three sessions: in the morning students meet in the design studio for discussion and critiques; after lunch they spend the afternoon on the construction site; and then after dinner they are back in studio for an evening period to continue designing. Design/build/design.

The course moves between schemes for an individual project and the actual work of collaborative construction. Between breakfast and lunch, students learn to draw, conceptualize, and develop their own schemes for a project they have brought with them. These projects range from house design to home renovation to explorations of careers in design/build. After lunch the afternoon's project—typically a small outbuilding—brings the class together in a community of building. "We use the built project to get a hands-on experience and give reality to the things we are doing in the studio." Though it is a different project, the building links with the designing: "We talk about joists, and then they work with joists; they draw studs and rafters, and in the afternoon we frame up the walls and roof." When students return to studio in the evening, clothes are still flaked with sawdust, ears might still ring with a saw cut's whine, and hands still grasp wood's mass and texture. Design/build/redesign.

Building in the afternoon complements morning and evening studio meetings, and nested within its process is another design/build feedback loop. Even field decisions for small details like rafter tail profiles carry significance in the course's learning process. During these four hours each afternoon, John works with students to learn tools, make necessary design decisions, obtain materials, and construct the project. They have nine days, or about thirty-six total hours, to complete the build. The client pays for materials, and in return receives free labor as well as John's design/build oversight and expertise. Necessarily small but often unique with idiosyncrasies at this scale, projects have included a chicken coop, a farm stand, a porch, small additions, the frame for a two-car garage, a recycling center's office, and a Lapland sleeping cabin.

As a typology for design/build, the shed lends itself to the course's utility and immediacy. It is a building type that is simple, repeatable, and efficient, with the directness of platform framing. John notes:

"The platform system works well. Most of the students in my class are going to encounter that type of framing, so I want them to be familiar with it when they go on to build something else. That system also gives a sense of layout and how construction is often all about repetition: do it; now do it again; do it again; do it again."

Permutations of the shed project have included a storage room for picnic tables, a space for a flatbread maker's sauce cauldron, a garden shed that stores firewood on one side and tools on the other, and an all-purpose spec shed for general storage. This latter type is built on skids to facilitate movement to a site once it is completed.

The sheds are typically eight by ten feet, and John has kept the total material budget at about $2,400 by using dimensioned boards from the local lumberyard and rough-sawn siding from the mill. The budget becomes a tool for understanding the project—allocating funds and making compromises if something breaks the budget. Kiln-dried wood is more expensive, so where do you make up the difference? Sometimes the size of the shed comes into play; a 6-by-8-foot building allows the studio to home in on a $30-per-square-foot cost.

John is patient and cares deeply about students' educational experiences. He begins the process of construction at a very slow pace to allow each student to acclimate to tools, materials, and the full-scale, full-on physicality of manual labor. But there are only nine workdays, so John finds it necessary at times to be autocratic, even "a little dictatorial"—though not at all in his nature—in order to give a sense of the "urgency," to clarify the project's "hierarchy," and to "move it along." The lesson here is that some things are more important than others.

Students arrive at a schematic design with program and basic parti sketch in the morning session on day three, and they are cutting joists and beginning to sheathe the floor deck in the afternoon session. John describes how students marvel at the subtle but remarkable change of elevation—twelve inches off the ground feels like a skyscraper! By the end of the first week, half of the walls are up, and students will usually begin laying out rafters.

John typically celebrates reaching the structure's highest point—the tradition of "topping out"—with a tree branch or piece of greenery, and the following week continues with rafters, roof and wall sheathing, windows and doors, and as many details as time allows. By Thursday afternoon, everyone gathers for the class photo. On Friday, in the studio, each student presents an individual project to the class, the teachers, and a few invited professionals. This presentation hones students' graphic and verbal skills as well as their ability to communicate intentions. They take these skills and the presentation home to their partners, their builders, their suppliers, and their friends, and they continue developing their project with the skills they have learned.

2
On the first afternoon, instructor Tom Virant describes the site and project to the class on the jobsite prepared by the owner.

3
An easel with sketchpad serves as a teaching aid for diagrams, calculations, drawings, and notes throughout the site construction.

4
The builder's level sets elevation heights for the foundation and floor framing.

5
The stadia pole provides vertical reference measurements.

6
Repetitive cuts allow students to practice tool use.

7
In Vermont, foundations rest below the 5-foot frost line. The chicken coop included 6x6 ground-contact-rated, pressure-treated posts in trenches that were back-filled with gravel for drainage.

8
Columns were wrapped in polyethylene to reduce the friction between posts and gravel during movement caused by frost heave.

9
Tom and John supervise decking to ensure that the rough-sawn lumber parallels the deck framing. Chicken wire below the decking protects against predators.

10
Deck framing proceeds in an open part of the site so that foundation work can continue simultaneously.

11
Preparing the wall panel.

12–13
Framing and moving a braced wall panel.

14
Framed structure for chicken coop. Horizontal blocking on 2-foot centers serves as nailers for the siding. Metal strapping provides diagonal bracing for the wall.

15
Assembling the doors and access hatches.

16
Attaching the wall sheathing.

17
Instructor David Bosco works with a student on the details for the operable hatches used for egg collection.

18
Completion of roof framing (John is holding the greenery that will be used to celebrate the "topping out").

19
Interior view of roof trusses and metal roofing.

20
Completed project before access
hatches are installed.

21
Installed access hatches.

22
The class photo on Thursday
afternoon marks the studio's last
day of work.

PROJECT INDEX

Project	Location	Date	Program	Instructor(s)
	Warren, Vermont	1980	Yestermorrow Design/Build School opens	
Popular Science Plywood Exercise and Renaissance Community Healing Center	Muncie, Indiana	1982	Ball State University (student won national competition)	Steve Badanes
Chicken Brooder and Suburban Renewal	Muncie, Indiana	1982	Ball State University (first-year studio)	Steve Badanes, Art Schaller, Linda Nelson Keane, Richard Sherida
Connell House Entry	Warren, Vermont	1982	Yestermorrow Design/Build School	Steve Badanes
Bamboo Deck and Pavilion	University of Miami courtyard (later moved to Metro Zoo, destroyed in Hurricane Andrew)	1984	University of Miami	Steve Badanes
Stairway to Nowhere [p. 69]	Architecture Hall, University of Washington campus, Seattle, Washington	1988	University of Washington	Steve Badanes, Donna Walter
Tool Shed	Danny Woo Community Garden, International District, Seattle, Washington	1989	University of Washington	Leslie Morishita, Brian Reading
Gould Hall Park	University District, Seattle, Washington	1990	University of Washington	Steve Badanes
Fremont Troll [p. 56]	Fremont neighborhood, Seattle, Washington	1990	Fremont Arts Council	Steve Badanes, Will Martin, Donna Walter, Ross Whitehead
Danny Woo Community Garden pig roast pit, vegetable washing and drying area, kiosks, compost bins, and seating [p. 21]	International District, Seattle, Washington	1990	University of Washington	Steve Badanes, Leslie Morishita, Andy Vanags
Gazebo and Deck	Waitsfield, Vermont	1990	Yestermorrow Design/Build School	John Ringel, Kathy Meyer, Brad Cook, Chris Jaquith
Millrace Pavilion	Eugene, Oregon	1991	University of Oregon	Steve Badanes, John Connell, Don Corner, Gunnar Hubbard, Dave Sellers
Garden Structures	Danny Woo Community Garden, International District, Seattle, Washington	1991	University of Washington	Steve Badanes, Leslie Morishita, Barry Onouye, Andy Vanags
Watchtower	Varkaus, Finland	1991	University of Technology, Otaniemi, Finland	Steve Badanes

Recycling as Architecture: Plywood Project, Light Fixture, Waterpiece	Muncie, Indiana	1991	Ball State University	Steve Badanes, John Ringel
Artist's Studio	Warren, Vermont	1991	Yestermorrow Design/ Build School	John Ringel, Kathy Meyer, Brad Cook, Chris Jaquith
Playground Structure (Warren Elementary School) [p. 70]	Warren, Vermont	1992	Yestermorrow Design/ Build School	John Ringel, Kathy Meyer, Chris Jaquith
Pavilion for America's Foundation	Tijuana, Mexico	1993	UC San Diego	Steve Badanes, Jim Brown
Hands on Materials	Tallahassee, Florida	1993	Florida A&M	Steve Badanes
Second-story addition to private residence	Warren, Vermont	1993	Yestermorrow Design/ Build School	John Ringel, Kathy Meyer, Gunnar Hubbard, Chris Jaquith
Canal Park seating areas and fire pit	Fremont neighborhood, Seattle	1994	University of Washington	Steve Badanes, Catherine Maggio
Solar Shower and Farmers' Market Bandstand [p. 122]	Warren, Vermont (Solar Shower is on Yestermorrow Design/Build School campus)	1994	Yestermorrow Design/ Build School	Steve Badanes, Kevin Ruel, Ron Cascio
Affordable Garage (Carport/ Shed #1)	Muncie, Indiana	1994	Yestermorrow Design/ Build School at Ball State	John Ringel, John Connell, Sylvia Smith, Jim Sanford, Gunnar Hubbard, Mac Rood (for both projects)
Affordable Garage (Carport/ Shed #2)	Muncie, Indiana	1994	Yestermorrow Design/ Build School at Ball State	
Porch addition to private residence	Warren, Vermont	1994	Yestermorrow Design/ Build School	John Ringel, Chris Jaquith, Kathy Meyer, Ned White
Experimental Education Unit Suspended Play Structures [p. 69]	University of Washington Health Science, Seattle, Washington	1995	University of Washington	Steve Badanes, Damon Smith
Alaska Outward Build	Talkeetna, Alaska	1995	University of Washington	Steve Badanes, Kim Brown, Joan Heaton, Rob Peña, Mark Stasik
Denise Louie Dragon Play Structure	Seattle, Washington	1995	Head Start	Steve Badanes, Joan Heaton, Linda Beaumont, Dave Robertson
Escuela San Lucas: Site and Garden Pavilion and Elementary School Buildings [p. 27]	Colonia San Lucas, Tejalpa, Morelos, Mexico	1995–97	University of Washington Mexico Design/Build	Steve Badanes, Sergio Palleroni, Tim Becker, Linda Beaumont, Margarette Leite, Rene Mancilla, Daniel Simons, Penelope West
Artists Cooperative Studio/ Gallery	Muncie, Indiana	1995	Yestermorrow Design/ Build School at Ball State	John Ringel, John Connell, Jim Sanford, Mac Rood, Diane Gayer, Gunnar Hubbard (for both projects)
Affordable Garage (Carport/ Shed #3)	Muncie, Indiana	1995	Yestermorrow Design/ Build School at Ball State	

Garage	Waitsfield, Vermont	1995	Yestermorrow Design/ Build School	John Ringel, Kathy Meyer, Chris Jaquith, Alan Holt
Timber Frame Art studio	Warren, Vermont	1995	Yestermorrow Design/ Build School	Steve Badanes, Steve Amstutz
Danny Woo Community Garden stairs, accessible gardens, and vegetable washing and drying deck	International District, Seattle, Washington	1996	University of Washington	Steve Badanes Penelope West
Affordable Garage (Carport/ Shed #4)	Muncie, Indiana	1996	Yestermorrow Design/ Build School at Ball State	John Ringel, Dianne Gayer, Mac Rood, Bill MaClay, Alisa Dworsky (for both projects)
White River Gateway Pavilion	Muncie, Indiana	1996	Yestermorrow Design/ Build School at Ball State	
Magic Mountain Daycare Center Story Time Pavilion [p. 30]	South Royalton, Vermont	1996	Yestermorrow Design/ Build School	Steve Badanes, Bill Bialosky
House Addition	Warren, Vermont	1996	Yestermorrow Design/ Build School	John Ringel
Experimental Education Unit Infant and Toddler Playcourt	University of Washington Health Science, Seattle, Washington	1997	University of Washington	Steve Badanes, Damon Smith, Scott Carr
Rock Point School Entry Stair	Burlington, Vermont	1997	Yestermorrow Design/ Build School	John Ringel, Joan Heaton, Alan Holt, Dave Robertson
Winooski Mill kiosks	Winooski, Vermont	1997	Yestermorrow Design/ Build School	Steve Badanes, Dave Robertson
Highland Gardens Community Garden: Pavilion and Work Area [p. 41]	Issaquah, Washington	1998	University of Washington	Steve Badanes, Damon Smith
Casa de Salud Malitzin	Tejalpa, Mexico	1998	University of Washington Mexico Design/Build	Steve Badanes, Sergio Palleroni, Rene Mancilla, Catalina Mojica
Guest Cabin on Yestermorrow campus	Warren, Vermont	1998	Yestermorrow Design/ Build School	John Ringel, Lisa Williams, Chris Jaquith
Phantom Theater Entry	Warren, Vermont	1998	Yestermorrow Design/ Build School	Steve Badanes, Bill Bialosky
Bradner Gardens Park East and South Entries, Trellis, Retaining Wall, and Footbridge [p. 37]	Mount Baker neighborhood, Seattle, Washington	1999	University of Washington	Steve Badanes, Damon Smith
Casa de Salud Malitzin	Tejalpa, Mexico	1999	University of Washington Mexico Design/Build	Steve Badanes, Sergio Palleroni, Rene Mancilla, Linda Beaumont, Jeff Hegg, Karen McCaughan
East Warren Schoolhouse Market Deck	East Warren, Vermont	1999	Yestermorrow Design/ Build School	John Ringel, John Pece, Kathy Meyer

Waitsfield Castle Playground Structure	Waitsfield Elementary School	1999	Yestermorrow Design/ Build School	Steve Badanes, Bill Bialosky
Bradner Gardens Park Entry and Pavilion [p. 37]	Mount Baker neighborhood, Seattle, Washington	2000	University of Washington	Steve Badanes, Damon Smith
Escuela Rosario Castellanos	Colonia Cuauhtémoc Càrdenas, Juitepec, Morelos, Mexico	2000	University of Washington Mexico Design/Build	Steve Badanes, Sergio Palleroni, Jim Adamson, Jason Manges
Porch Roof of East Warren Schoolhouse Market [p. 122]	East Warren, Vermont	2000	Yestermorrow Design/ Build School	John Ringel, John Pece, Kathy Meyer
Public Toilet Porto-let Enclosure	Lareau Farm Park, Warren, Vermont	2000	Yestermorrow Design/ Build School	Steve Badanes
Library	Abrafo-Odumasi, Ghana	2000	Miami University	Steve Badanes, Gail Della-Piana
Trellis, Equipment Sheds, Amphitheater and seating [p.37]	T. T. Minor Elementary School, Seattle, Washington	2001	University of Washington	Steve Badanes, Damon Smith, Jason Davis
Urban Organic Agricultural Center [p. 27]	Havana, Cuba	2001	University of Washington	Steve Badanes, Jim Adamson, Sergio Palleroni, Linda Beaumont, Jason Manges
Biblioteca Pública Municipal Juana de Asbaje y Ramirez [p.18]	Colonia Joya de Agua, Juitepec, Morelos, Mexico	2001	University of Washington Mexico Design/Build	Steve Badanes, Jim Adamson, Sergio Palleroni, Linda Beaumont, Jason Manges, Jim Garrett, Oscar Mendoza
Storage Shed at Secret Location	Prickly Mountain, Vermont	2001	Yestermorrow Design/ Build School	John Ringel, John Pece, Art Schaller
Skatium Warming Hut	Waitsfield, Vermont	2001	Yestermorrow Design/ Build School	Steve Badanes
Concession stand and ticket booths for university soccer field [p. 63]	Milwaukee, Wisconsin	2001	University of Wisconsin–Milwaukee	Jim Adamson, Steve Badanes, John Ringel, Mark Keane
Performance and Play Stage Minor	T. T. Minor Elementary School, Seattle, Washington	2002	University of Washington	Steve Badanes, Damon Smith
U.S.A. Pavilion Dormitory	Auroville, India	2002	University of Washington	Steve Badanes, Jim Adamson, Sergio Palleroni, Jason Manges, Mark Merkelbach, Sharon Khosla
Library reading pavilion	Abrafo-Odumasi, Ghana	2002	Miami University	Jim Adamson, Gail Della-Piana
Montpelier Parks Office and Visitors' Center	Hubbard Park, Montpelier, Vermont	2002	Yestermorrow Design/ Build School	John Ringel, Hilary Harris, John Pece, Lisa Williams, Fred Oesch

Four Corners Bus Shelter (also known as East Warren Bus Stop Shelter) [p. 51]	East Warren, Vermont	2002	Yestermorrow Design/ Build School	Steve Badanes, Bill Bialosky
Covered Marketplace, Plaza [p. 27]	Abrafo-Odumasi, Ghana	2003	Miami University	Jim Adamson, Gail Della-Piana
Composting toilet [p. 27]	Abrafo-Odumasi, Ghana	2003	Miami University	Jim Adamson, Gail Della-Piana
Danny Woo Community Garden New Face Project [p. 64]	International District, Seattle, Washington	2003	University of Washington	Steve Badanes, Damon Smith, Ariel Kemp
Unidad Basica de Rehabilitacion: Clinic for handicapped children	Xochitepec, Morelos, Mexico	2003	University of Washington Mexico Design/Build	Steve Badanes, Jim, Adamson, Sergio Palleroni, Jason Manges, Mark Merkelbach, Christina Eichbaum Merkelbach
American Flatbread Shed for Sauce Cauldron	Waitsfield, Vermont	2003	Yestermorrow Design/ Build School	John Ringel, Tom Virant, Kathy Meyer
Verd-Mont Trailer Park Rocket [p. 51]	Warren, Vermont	2003	Yestermorrow Design/ Build School	Jim Adamson, Steve Badanes, Bill Bialosky
Small Cabin	Warren, Vermont	2003	Yestermorrow Design/ Build School	Jim Adamson, Dan Johnson
Noji Commons [pp.105–110]	Noji Gardens, Rainier Valley, Washington	2004	University of Washington	Steve Badanes, Damon Smith, Sam Batchelor Molly Cherney, Craig Hollow
Solar Kitchen and Dining for Juan Maria Morelos Elementary School [p. 116]	Colonia San Jose, Morelos, Mexico	2004	University of Washington Mexico Design/Build	Jim Adamson, Sergio Palleroni, Jason Manges, Peter Spruance
Hartshorn Farmstand	Waitsfield, Vermont	2004	Yestermorrow Design/ Build School	John Ringel, Tom Virant, Hilary Harris
Armadillo Structure for Patch Adams' Gesundheit Institute: The Chrysalis [p. 50]	West Virginia	2004	Yestermorrow Design/ Build School	Jim Adamson, Steve Badanes, Bill Bialosky, Dave Sellers
Screened porch addition	Warren, Vermont	2004	Yestermorrow Design/ Build School	Jim Adamson, Dan Johnson
Arboretum Bandshell	Ann Arbor, Michigan	2004	University of Michigan	Steve Badanes
Arboretum Sunhouse [p. 19]	Washington State Arboretum, Seattle, Washington	2005	University of Washington	Steve Badanes, Damon Smith, Stewart Germain
Community Center and Library Remodel	Lao Highland Association, Seattle, Washington	2005	University of Washington	Steve Badanes, Dave Sarti
Mad River Path Trail Shelter [p. 118]	Warren, Vermont	2005	Yestermorrow Design/ Build School	Jim Adamson, Steve Badanes, Bill Bialosky

House Addition	Northfield, Vermont	2005	Yestermorrow Design/ Build School	John Ringel, Tom Virant, Kathy Meyer
Forest pavilion	Warren, Vermont	2005	Yestermorrow Design/ Build School	Jim Adamson, Dan Johnson, Mark Three Stars
Sustainable housing prototypes for indigenous people from the Sonora Desert	Obregon, Mexico	2005	University of Texas at Austin, Design/Build Mexico	Jim Adamson, Sergio Palleroni, Peter Spruance
Sustainable rain screen walls for a hot, humid climate	National Taipei University of Technology, Taiwan	2005	National Taipei University of Technology	Jim Adamson, Sergio Palleroni, Peter Spruance
Mobile Writers' Studio [p. 28]	Shelburne Farms, Vermont	2006	Yestermorrow Design/ Build School	Jim Adamson, Steve Badanes, Bill Bialosky
Mount Baker Gateways and Waiting Shelter	Mount Baker neighborhood, Issaquah, Washington	2006	University of Washington	Steve Badanes, Thomas Schaer, Stewart Germain, Dave Lipe
Wilson Recycling Depot	Central Vermont Solid Waste District (recycled as sleeping cabin at Yestermorrow)	2006	Yestermorrow Design/ Build School	John Ringel, Eyrich Stauffer, Kathy Meyer, Marc Chalom, Linda Lloyd
Small outbuilding for local school	Warren, Vermont	2006	Yestermorrow Design/ Build School	Jim Adamson, Dan Johnson
Katrina Furniture Project	New Orleans, Louisiana	2006	University of Texas at Austin	Jim Adamson, Sergio Palleroni, Peter Spruance, Sandor Pratt
Danny Woo Community Garden Gathering Place [p. 120]	International District, Seattle, Washington	2007	University of Washington	Steve Badanes, Chad Robertson, Dave Lipe, Brett Smith
Eco Pavilion	Brightwater Sewage Treatment Facility, Woodinville, Washington	2007	University of Washington	Jim Adamson, Steve Badanes
Picnic Table Storage Shed for Evergreen Place Senior Center [p. 111]	Waitsfield, Vermont	2007	Yestermorrow Design/ Build School	John Ringel, Kathy Meyer, Hilary Harris, Jeremy Warms
Mobile Farmstand: Veggie- mobile [p. 21]	Shelburne Farms, Vermont	2007	Yestermorrow Design/ Build School	Jim Adamson, Steve Badanes, Bill Bialosky
Atlantic Center for the Arts Visiting Artist Pavilion	New Smyrna Beach, Florida	2007	Atlantic Center for the Arts	Steve Badanes, Jim Adamson, Bill Sanders
Seattle Tilth Tool Shed	Seattle, Washington	2008 (first part)	University of Washington	Steve Badanes, Chad Robertson, Gus Sinsheimer
Lao Highland Association Community Pavilion [p. 36]	Seattle, Washington	2008 (second part)	University of Washington	Steve Badanes, Chad Robertson, Gus Sinsheimer
Garden/Visitor Pavilion and Laundry Station for Maternity Clinic [p. 26]	Perquin, El Salvador	January 2008	MIT	Jim Adamson, Reinhardt Goethert, Dave Sellers, Ethan Lacy, and Zach Lamb

Cafe remodel, exhibition gallery, signage, and portable exhibit system	Montreal, Canada	March 2008	McGill University	Steve Badanes, Lian Chang
House Addition	Northfield, Vermont	2008	Yestermorrow Design/ Build School	John Ringel, Tom Virant, Kathy Meyer
Mad River Path Trailhead Kiosk [p. 32]	Warren School, Warren, Vermont	2008	Yestermorrow Design/ Build School	Jim Adamson, Steve Badanes, Bill Bialosky
Casa de Pollo (chicken coop)	Warren, Vermont	2008	Yestermorrow Design/ Build School	Jim Adamson, Dan Johnson
Wellspring Family Services Playhouse and Living Fence [p. 52]	Seattle, Washington	2009	University of Washington	Steve Badanes, Chad Robertson, Travis Anderson
Entrance Plaza to Amun Shea Elementary School [p. 23]	Perquin, El Salvador	2009	MIT	Jim Adamson, Charles Mathis, Ethan Lacy, Zach Lamb
Motes Orchid Pavilion [p. 59]	Redland, Florida	2009	University of Miami	Jim Adamson, Rocco Ceo
Tiny Cabin	Warren, Vermont	2009	Yestermorrow Design/ Build School	John Ringel, Tom Virant, Kathy Meyer
Wheeler Brook Apartments Picnic Pavilion [p. 122]	Warren, Vermont	2009	Yestermorrow Design/ Build School	Jim Adamson, Steve Badanes, Bill Bialosky
Individual and communal work areas	Portland, Oregon	2009	Oregon College of Art and Craft and Pacific Northwest College of Art	Steve Badanes, Laura Yeats, J. P. Reuer
Helping Link Community Center Revitalization [p. 87]	Seattle, Washington	2010	University of Washington	Steve Badanes, Chad Robertson, Ashley Muse
Rural Kitchen [see "Cases"]	Ampil Peum Elementary School, Siem Reap, Cambodia	2010	MIT	Jim Adamson, Ethan Lacy, Zach Lamb, John Ochsendorf
Lapin Tupa (Lapland Sleeping Cabin)	Undisclosed location in Vermont	2010	Yestermorrow Design/ Build School	John Ringel, Kathy Meyer, Tom Virant, Ben Chamberlain
Hubbard Park Compost Privy	Montpelier, Vermont	2010	Yestermorrow Design/ Build School	Jim Adamson, Steve Badanes, Bill Bialosky
Mobile PermaKitchen: teaching and processing kitchen for Earth Learning Institute [p. 41]	Miami, Florida	2010–11	University of Miami	Jim Adamson, Rocco Ceo, Ralph Provisero, Mike Arnspiger
El Centro de la Raza outdoor classrooms and community circle [p. 19]	Santos Rodriguez Memorial Park, Seattle, Washington	2011	University of Washington	Steve Badanes, Jake LaBarre, Magda Celinska, Jack DeBlauwe
Deane Nature Preserve Pedestrian Bridge [p. 123]	Poultney, Vermont	2011	Yestermorrow Design/ Build School	Jim Adamson, Steve Badanes, Bill Bialosky

Firewood and Garden Shed [p. 25]	Huntington, Vermont	2011	Yestermorrow Design/ Build School	John Ringel, Kathy Meyer, Rob Maddox, Lizbeth Moniz
Everglades Eco-Tent [see p. 38]	Everglades National Park, Flamingo, Florida	Spring 2012	University of Miami	Jim Adamson, Rocco Ceo
Urban Farm Supershed [see "Cases"]	Center for Urban Horticulture at University of Washington Botanic Gardens	2012	University of Washington	Steve Badanes, Jake LaBarre, Ji Shon
Chicken Coop and Garden Shed	Waitsfield, Vermont	2012	Yestermorrow Design/ Build School	John Ringel, David Bosco, Tom Virant
Composting Toilet Structure [p. 51]	Maple sugar area, Shelburne Farms, Vermont	2012	Yestermorrow Design/ Build School	Jim Adamson, Steve Badanes, Bill Bialosky, Miriam Gee
Guara Ki (Place of Earth Spirit) Eco Farm Rural Bathroom Facility [p. 28]	Homestead, Florida	Spring 2013	University of Miami	Jim Adamson, Rocco Ceo
Room for a Forest [p. 113]	Beacon Food Forest, Seattle, Washington	2013	University of Washington	Steve Badanes, Jake LaBarre, Kevin Lang
Spec Shed	Yestermorrow Design/Build School Tennis Court	2013	Yestermorrow Design/ Build School	John Ringel, Kathy Meyer, Mark Billian
Composting Toilet Structure [p. 51]	Market Garden, Shelburne Farms, Vermont	2013	Yestermorrow Design/ Build School	Jim Adamson, Steve Badanes, Bill Bialosky, Miriam Gee
Children's Garden Neighborhood Cookery [p. 54]	Danny Woo Community Garden, Seattle, Washington	2014	University of Washington	Steve Badanes, Jake LaBarre, Miriam Gee, Jena Restad (TA), Scott Viloria (TA)
Shed	Warren, Vermont	2014	Yestermorrow Design/ Build School	John Ringel, Kathy Meyer, Rob Maddox, Art Schaller
Outdoor Classroom and Playhouse	Fayston Elementary School, Fayston, Vermont	2014	Yestermorrow Design/ Build School	Jim Adamson, Steve Badanes, Bill Bialosky, Miriam Gee
Outdoor classroom for organic coffee farm	Turrialba, Costa Rica	2014	Build Lightly / Costa Rica	Jim Adamson, Steve Badanes, Miriam Gee, Luke Perry
Coffee Kiosk [p. 33]	University of Miami Campus	Fall 2014	University of Miami	Jim Adamson, Rocco Ceo
Urban Preschool Greenhouse	Woodland Park Community Preschool at Fremont Baptist Church	Spring 2015	University of Washington	Steve Badanes, Jake LaBarre, Miriam Gee, Jason Glover (TA)
Footbridge for Laraway Youth and Family Services	Johnson, Vermont	2015	Yestermorrow Design/ Build School	Jim Adamson, Steve Badanes, Bill Bialosky
Equipment Shed for WMRW Community Radio tower	Warren, Vermont	2015	Yestermorrow Design/ Build School	John Ringel, Kathy Meyer, Rob Maddox

Jim Adamson at MIT

Entrance Plaza to Amun Shea

Coinstructor: Charles Mathis; Organizers: Ethan Lacy, Zach Lamb; Students: Jordan Allison, Deborah Buelow, Keith Case, Dorian Dargan, Andrey Dimitrov, Emily Lo, Leslie Lok, Sung Mi Kim, Yushiro Okamoto, Harriet Provine, Alice Rosenberg, Jason Tapia

Rural Kitchen

See project credits in "Cases."

Jim Adamson and Rocco Ceo at University of Miami

Motes Orchid Pavilion

Teaching Assistant: Ralph Provisero; Students: Robert Douglas, Melissa Harrison, Tang-Ning Kuo, Jessica Corter, Courtney Webster, Luna Bernfest, Claudia Acuna, Aramis Camacho, Lamar Rollins, Amanda Del Rio, Eric Brown, Billy King, Jessica Rausch

Mobile Permakitchen

Students: Thomas Johnson, Hassan Bagheri, Mai Oizumi, Etai Timnai, Nick Marinos, Ryan Coffield, Eric Ross, David Chessrown, Carol Santana, Ashley Walton, Jenna Chandler, Karl Landsteiner

Bathroom Facility

Students: Robert Allison, Nestor Arguello, Sinead Camilo, Drew Dent, Miles Glover, Francisco Jimenez, Kristen Meyer, Ariana Ragusa, Amanda Rosenfeld, Monica Socorro, Ma Zheng, Jie Zhu

Eco-Tent

Students: Glenn Laaspere, Giancarlo Belledonne, Carlo Guzman, Kelly Sawyna, Meagan Sippel, Catherine O'Sullivan, Michael Galea, Violet Battat, Ruslana Makarenko, Sam Vana, Luan Hao

Coffee Kiosk

Students: Giuliano D'Arrigo, Stacy Griffith, Andrea Gonzales-Rebull, James Harris, Zhengrong Hu, Brenna Johnson, Victor Kroh, Taylor Lichteberger, Emma May, Lauren O'Halloran, Adam Raiffe, Angelica Marie Tavarez, Hiwot Tefera

Steve Badanes at the University of Washington

Stairway to Nowhere

Teaching Assistant: Donna Walter; Students: John Bettman, Jeff Floor, Brooke Kelly, Marty Koenigs, Nora Liu, Heikki Lonka, Ted Nash, Andrew Smith, Bill Soules, Nat Tilahun, Julie Warrick, Karl Westerback

Canal Park Seating

Coinstructor: Catherine Maggio; Students: Dave Bonewitz, Catherine Cook, Wayne Evers, Anna Hagenblad, Michael Jak, Claire Johnson, Matti Kajansinkko, Markus Kolb, Rowena Lee, Tracy Margel, Susan McNabb, Daren Overstreet

Experimental Education Unit Suspended Play Structures

Coinstructor: Damon Smith; Students: Gerald Beltran, Arthur Cole, Craig Compton, Kay Compton, Gabe Hajiani, Karen Hovde, Gregory Kewish, Jennifer Paris, Barley Phillips, Xylon Saltzman, John Smith, Tobin Thompson, Audra Tuskes

Danny Woo Community Garden Stairs, Accessible Gardens, and Other Garden Structures

Coinstructor: Penelope West; Students: Jennifer Caudle, Patricia Dunleavy, Susan Elkan, Huyen Hoang, Mike Mackie, Julia Park, Laila Podra, Susan Sprague, Jay Thoman, Sylvia Vierthaler, Margaret Wong

Experimental Education Unit Infant and Toddler Playcourt

Coinstructors: Scott Carr, Damon Smith; Students: Jim Baurichter, John Cashman, Erik Fish, Hans Hansen, Mike Herbst, Young Kim, Kirk MacGowan, Kim Magnussen, Chris Patterson, Erika Price, Derek Rae, Trevor Schaaf

Highland Gardens Community Garden: Pavilion and Work Area

Coinstructor: Damon Smith; Students: Steve Brown, Ian Butcher, Ken Camarata, Marlene Chen, Sean Fleming, Jay Greening, Mark Jones, Jeffrey Kebschull, Angela Melsner, Doug Norem, Ron Pizarro, Lisa Youk

Bradner Gardens Park East and South Entries, Trellis, Retaining Wall, and Footbridge

Coinstructor: Damon Smith; Students: Jeff Boone, Julie Chen, Sam Chung, Stewart Germain, Chain Jingjang, Julie Matsumoto, Ryan Rhodes, Michael Smith, Daria Supp, Michael Weller

Bradner Gardens Park Entry and Pavilion

Coinstructor: Damon Smith; Students: Charla Bear, Todd Biggerman, Chris Countryman, Julie Elledge, Michael Godfried, Dave Lipe, Trygve Oye, Alex Pheiffer, Daniel Poei, Chris Samujh, Errett Schneider, Winnie So, Todd Wolf

Trellis, Equipment Sheds, Amphitheater and seating

Coinstructors: Damon Smith, Jason Davis; Students: Joshua Abbell, Erica Burns, Renee Del Gaudio, Jay Greening, Thea Haberstetzer, Lai Luig Kong, Aaron Pleskac, Andres Quintero, John Shack, Matthew Somerton, Natalie Thomas, Michael Wells, Sara Wilder, Matthew Woodhouse-Kent

Performance and Play Stage

Coinstructor: Damon Smith; Students: Jim Beckett, Kari Callahan, Mark Davis, Roy Hague, Ariel Kemp, Collin Kwan, Chen Yi Lee, Dan Malone, Rene Nishakawa, Brian Purdy, Mike Rausch, Jonas Weber, Lea Yang, Mei Yee Yap, Daisuke Zaoya

Danny Woo Community Garden New Face Project

Coinstructor: Damon Smith; Teaching Assistant: Ariel Kemp; Students: Kevin Armstrong, Kaitlin Barth, Sam Batchelor, Andrew Billings, Kristen Billings, Rebecca Dixon, Jon Fukutomi, Patrick Kuo, Zenifer Macalino, Greg Miller, Nora Ng, Susan Olmsted, Arnold Lee Ramoso, Greg Shiffler, Jessie Temple, Jennifer Uh, Alison Waldsmith, Ilva Wilson

Noji Commons

Coinstructor: Damon Smith; Teaching Assistants: Sam

Batchellor, Molly Cherney, Craig Hollow; Students: Cedric Barringer, Dave Biddle, Jaqueline Bui, Tim Carter, David Chiefetz, Mike Freeman, Mark Haizlip, Zach Ham, Richard Jackman, John Kirk, Morgan McIntosh, Ryan Peck, Yvgenia Podvysotska, Erin Sonntag, Greg Squires, Laurie Stallings

Washington Park Arboretum Sunhouse

Coinstructor: Damon Smith; Teaching Assistant: Stewart Germain; Students: Angela Berry, Juli Garzon, Pete Hess, Julie Hong, Scott Kuchta, Kyle Larson, Joann Lee, Kirk Mcdonald, Dave Marchetti, Lisa Massingill, Byron Nesvog, Shawn Rafferty, Haipeng Ren, Chad Robertson, Ashley Vail, Nik Williams

Community Center and Library Remodel

Coinstructor: Dave Sarti; Students: Carl Baker, Curtis Names, Dawn Robinette, Travis Bell, Kevin Robinson, Mitali Advikar, Shanna Bodle, Carlos Gimenez, Meredith Keller, Jocie White, Mark Ronish

Mount Baker Gateways and Waiting Shelter

Coinstructor: Thomas Schaer; Teaching Assistants: Stewart Germain, Dave Lipe; Students: Mary Chan, Kevin Clement, Jeff Crawford, Elisabeta Curea, Lauren Eck, Kenji Hoshide, Nanika Lee, Sam McPhetres, Sam Mesikepp, Yeuk Ng, Vu Nguyen, Davila Parker-Garcia, Sokhour Seng, Megan Sheets, Denise Thompson, Tiffany Wang

Danny Woo Community Garden Gathering Place

Coinstructor: Chad Robertson;

Teaching Assistants: Dave Lipe, Brett Smith; Students: Caroline Davis, Rachel Dentel, Derek Enders, Leslie Lane, Charla Lemoine, Ana Levan, Adrian Parke, Erin Paysse, Chris Potter, J. J. Powell, Sam Scarmado, Mary Seng, Gus Sinsheimer, Loc Tran, Bryan Vanderlugt, Ryan Wong

Lao Highland Association Community Pavilion

Coinstructor: Chad Robertson; Teaching Assistant: Warren "Gus" Sinsheimer; Students: Julia Lindgren, Rachel Abolofia, Gia Mugford, Amanda Reed, Dan Lazarek, Travis Anderson, Jen Brooks, Jeff Benton, Rie Shintani, Sam Nicklay, Audrey Juliana, Anne Gantt, Ian Hamm, Ryan Zamora, Claire Gear, Adrienne Wicks, Tiffany Rattray

Wellspring Family Services Playhouse and Living Fence

Coinstructor: Chad Robertson; Teaching Assistant: Travis Anderson; Students: Erin Anderson, Laura Brown, Magdalena Celinska, Joe David, Laura Granados, Scott Hanson, Jeff Hudak, Jack Hunter, Justin Lui, Ashley Muse, Chris Pineo, Matt Quijano, Zach Reed, Gus Starkey, Ted Wegrich, Josh Williamson

Helping Link Community Center Revitalization

Coinstructor: Chad Robertson; Teaching Assistant: Ashley Muse; Students: Amy Monsen, Bragdon Shields, Chris Wong, Eryn Gaul, Marty Brennan, Mary Fialko, Minh Nguyen, Natalie Gualy, Nina Aidas, Paul Ramey, Jack DeBlauw, Jennifer Richter, Jesse Belknap, John Angle, Jon Haufe, Lily Schwering, Steve Shatswell, Titus Uomoto

El Centro de la Raza outdoor classrooms and community circle

Coinstructor: Jake LaBarre; Teaching Assistants: Magdalena Celinska, Jack Deblauw; Students: Aaron Allan, Anne Bjerre, Mike Blackburn, Amanda Chenowith, Erin Feeney, Jesus Garcia, Jeff Hyslop, Todd Illy, Maria-Therese Kazantzidou, Jeff Ko, Sam Kraft, James Moehring, Jay Ranaweera, Ji Shon, Doug Smith, Adam Stoeckle, Juan Vergara, Scott Viloria

Urban Farm Supershed

Coinstructor: Jake LaBarre; Teaching Assistant: Ji Shon; Students: Giselle Altea, Emily Aune, Jordan Bell, Jessica Fabro, Wendy Fan, Louisa Galassini, Tera Hatfield, Kelly Hogg, Kevin Lang, Carolyn LeCompte, Erin McDade, David Neuville, Arnulfo Ramirez, Jason Sawyer, Tyrel Sullivan, Christopher Yee, Joseph Wessinger

Room For A Forest

Coinstructor: Jake LaBarre; Teaching Assistant: Kevin Lang; Students: Ben Ahearn, Jessica Bailey, Kyle Boyd, Bryan Brooks, Erica Brissenden, Grace Crofoot, April Kelley, Andrew Mariano, Emily Perchilk, Jena Restad, Jeff Sandler, Sigrid "Sam" Santos, Bennett Sapin, Evan Schmidt, Amelia Simoncelli, Scott Viloria, Cameron Wu, Angela Yang; Volunteer: Jake Ehlers

Children's Garden Neighborhood Cookery

Coinstructor: Jake LaBarre; Teaching Assistants: Jena Restad, Scott Viloria; Project Manager: Miriam Gee; Students: Chad Bailey, Ryan Cox, Brian Gallego, Jason Gover,

Peter Gray, Jorge Guzman, Ibet Hernandez, Mariam Hovhannisyan, Dorris Hwang, Olof Jondelius, Araceli Lopez, Joe Mariarity, Preston Mossing, Anna Pajulo, Kristen Strobel, Lily Sun, Tanya Trongham, Axel Zedell

Urban Preschool Greenhouse

Coinstructor: Jake LaBarre; Teaching Assistant: Jason Gover; IDP Volunteer: Jorge Guzman; Students: Mikhail Balusyuk, Virginia Bradbury, Jordan Cowhig, Gabe Helmes, Connor Irick, Zeke Jones, Reed Kelly, Joao Leite, Jule Martinelli, Nicole McKernan, Tanya Nachia, Caitlin Omai, Lexi Paparo, Sam Parish, Keegan Raleigh, Rauland Schaat, Nile Van Westrienen, Qisheng Wen

Jim Adamson, Steve Badanes, and John Ringel at Yestermorrow Design/Build School

Public Interest Design/Build Classes

Coinstructors: Bill Bialosky, Miriam Gee
Home Design/Build Classes
Coinstructors: Kathy Meyer, Tom Virant, Rob Maddox, David Bosco, Chris Jaquith, John Pece, Art Schaller

Thanks to: The full-time staff and interns at Yestermorrow for making these classes possible since 1980; the citizens of Vermont and the local communities for their support and for providing local projects; and the hundreds of students who have taken classes and supported the school.

FURTHER READING

Architecture for Humanity, ed. *Design Like You Give a Damn: Architectural Responses to Humanitarian Crises.* New York: Metropolis Books, 2006.

Architecture for Humanity, ed. *Design Like You Give a Damn (2): Building Change from the Ground Up.* New York: Harry N. Abrams, 2012.

Bell, Bryan, ed. *Good Deeds, Good Design: Community Service Through Architecture.* New York: Princeton Architectural Press, 2004.

Bryan Bell and Katie Wakeford, eds. *Expanding Architecture: Design as Activism.* New York: Metropolis Books, 2008.

Bizios, Georgia and Katie Wakeford. *Bridging the Gap: Public-Interest Architectural Internships.* Raleigh, NC: Lulu Press, 2011.

Carpenter, William J. and Dan Hoffman. *Learning by Building: Design and Construction in Architectural Education.* New York: Van Nostrand Reinhold, 1997.

Cohen, Janie. *Architectural Improvisation: A History of Vermont's Design/Build Movement 1964–1977.* Burlington, VT: University of Vermont Press and Robert Hull Fleming Museum, 2008.

Crosbie, Michael J. *The Jersey Devil Design/Build Book.* Salt Lake City: Peregrine Smith Books, 1985.

Dean, Andrea Oppenheimer. *Rural Studio: Samuel Mockbee and an Architecture of Decency.* New York: Princeton Architectural Press, 2002.

Dean, Andrea Oppenheimer. *Proceed and Be Bold: Rural Studio After Samuel Mockbee.* New York: Princeton Architectural Press, 2005.

Escher, Gustav and John Ringel. *Bubble Dorm Working Paper No. 1: Research and design of an inflatable enclosure as residence.* Submitted to the Student Housing Cooperative at Princeton University, November 1970.

Fathy, Hassan. *Architecture for the Poor: An Experiment in Rural Egypt.* Chicago: University of Chicago Press, 1973.

Freear, Andrew and Elena Barthel. *Rural Studio at Twenty: Designing and Building in Hale County, Alabama.* New York: Princeton Architectural Press, 2014.

Geddes, Robert. *Fit: An Architect's Manifesto.* Princeton: Princeton University Press, 2012.

Geddes, Robert and Bernard Spring. *A Study of Education for Environmental Design: A Report by Princeton University for the American Institute of Architects*, Princeton University, December 1967.

Gjerston, W. Geoff. "House Divided: Challenges to Design/Build from Within," in *Proceedings of the Association of Collegiate Schools of Architecture*, ACSA Fall Conference, 2011.

Hardin, Mary C., Richard Eribes, and Charles (Corky) Poster, eds. *From the Studio to the Streets: Service-learning in Planning and Architecture.* Sterling, VA: Stylus, 2006.

Hayes, Richard W. *The Yale Building Project: The First 40 Years.* New Haven: Yale School of Architecture, 2007.

Hou, Jeffrey, Julie M. Johnson and Laura J. Lawson. *Greening Cities, Growing Communities: Learning from Seattle's Community Gardens.* Seattle: University of Washington Press, 2009.

Krauel, Jacabo. *Inflatable Art, Architecture, and Design.* Barcelona: Links Books, 2014.

Labatut, Jean. Quoted in William S. McClanahan, "Professor Jean Labatut, Noted Modern Architect, Comments on Novel Church, Experimental Lab," *The Daily Princetonian*, 15 May 1952, page 4.

Lepik, Andres. *Small Scale, Big Change: New Architectures of Social Engagement.* New York: Museum of Modern Art, 2010.

MacKay-Lyons, Brian. *Ghost: Building and Architectural Vision.* New York: Princeton Architectural Press, 2008.

Brian MacKay-Lyons. Robert McCarter, ed. *Local Architecture: Building Place, Craft, and Community.* New York: Princeton Architectural Press, 2015.

Macy, Christine. *Free Lab: Design-Build Projects from the School of Architecture, Dalhousie University, Canada, 1991-2006.* Halifax, N.S.: Tuns Press, 2008.

Moos, David and Gail Trechsel, eds. *Samuel Mockbee and The Rural Studio: Community Architecture.* New York: Birmingham Museum of Art, 2003.

Ochsner, Jeffrey. *Furniture Studio: Materials, Craft, and Architecture.* Seattle: University of Washington Press, 2012.

Ockman, Joan, ed. *Architecture School: Three Centuries of Educating Architects in North America.* Cambridge, MA: MIT Press; Washington, DC: Association of Collegiate Schools of Architecture, 2012.

Palleroni, Sergio and Christina Eichbaum Merkelbach. *Studio at Large: Architecture in Service of Global Communities.* Seattle: University of Washington Press, 2004.

Pearson, Jason. *University-Community Design Partnerships: Innovations in Practice.* Washington, D.C.: NEA, 2002.

Pendleton-Jullian, Ann M. *The Road Is Not a Road and the Open City, Ritoque, Chile.* Cambridge, MA: MIT Press, 1996.

Piedmont-Palladino, Susan and Mark Alden Branch. *Devil's Workshop: 25 Years of Jersey Devil Architecture.* New York: Princeton Architectural Press, 1997.

Quale, John D. *Sustainable, Affordable, Prefab: The ecoMOD Project.* Charlottesville, VA: University of Virginia Press, 2012.

Salvadori, Mario. *Building: From Caves to Skyscrapers.* New York: Atheneum, 1979.

Salvadori, Mario. *The Art of Construction: Projects and Principles for Beginning Engineers and Architects.* Chicago: Chicago Review Press, 2000.

Smith, Cynthia E. *Design for the Other 90%.* New York: Smithsonian, Cooper-Hewitt, National Design Museum, 2007.

Steen, Bill, Athena Steen, and Eiko Komatsu. *Built By Hand: Vernacular Buildings Around the World.* Salt Lake City: Gibbs Smith, 2003.

Taylor, Jeff. *Tools of the Trade: The Art and Craft of Carpentry.* San Francisco: Chronicle Books, 1996.

Journals and magazines: *Fine Homebuilding, Fine Woodworking, Yankee Magazine's Forgotten Art of Building, Journal of Light Construction,* and *Whole Earth Catalog.*

Websites

Jersey Devil
www.jerseydevildesignbuild.com

University of Washington
Neighborhood
Design/Build Studio
ndbs.be.washington.edu

Yestermorrow Design/Build School
yestermorrow.org

"Jersey Devil says" icon:
Ed Sheetz

Speak of the Devil
Figs. 01, 07: Charlie Hailey; Figs. 02, 17–20: Jersey Devil Archives; 03, 05–06, 11–14, 23–24: Steve Badanes; 04: John Senzer, courtesy Jersey Devil Archives; 08: Mudd Manuscript Library, Princeton University, Historical Photograph Collection, Campus Life Series (AC112), Box MP 94, Image No. 1913; 09: Jean Labatut Collection, Princeton University School of Architecture Archive; 10: John Ringel, courtesy Jersey Devil Archives; 15–16: Gus Escher and John Ringel, Bubble Dorm Working Paper No. 1 (1970); 21: Jim Adamson; 22, 25–26: Steve Badanes, courtesy UW CBE Visual Resources Collection; 27–28: NDBS Archives.

Groundwork
01–02: Steve Badanes; 03, 05, 29: Joe McKay; 04: Ethan Lacy; 06: Mudd Manuscript Library, Princeton Bulletin, October 19, 1992, vol. 82, no. 6; 07: Kathy Meyer; 08, 14, 17–19, 24–28, 31: Steve Badanes; 09: Jim Adamson; 10–11: Jersey Devil Archives; 12, 20: NDBS Archives; 13: Jared Polesky; 15–16, 30, 32: Jim Adamson, Rocco Ceo; 21–23: Amanda Reed.

Toolbox
02–03, 05–08, 16–17, 21, 28–30, 33–38, 44–46, 71, 73–75, 80, 92: NDBS Archives; 04, 19–20, 24–27, 31–32, 39–40, 43, 48–49, 62–66, 78, 83, 86–91: Jim Adamson, Rocco Ceo; 09, 12–13, 22, 42, 70, 85: Steve Badanes; 10, 18: UW Mexico Design/Build Archives, courtesy UW CBE Visual Resources Collection; 11: Steve Badanes and Jim Adamson; 14–15, 41, 54: Jim Adamson; 23, 56 (right): UW CBE Visual Resources Collection; 47: Kathy Meyer; 51, 58: Jersey Devil Archives; 52: Josh Polansky; 53, 55, 59, 68–69: Steve Badanes, UW CBE Visual Resources Collection; 56 (left): Charlie Hailey; 57: Bill Sanders; 60: Mary Levin, UW CBE Visual Resources Collection; 61, 76: Yestermorrow Archives; 72: C. Brouwer et al, Training Manual No. 2: Elements of Topographic Surveying, United Nations FAO Land and Water Division; 77: Willis H. Wagner, Modern Carpentry, New York: Goodheart-Willcox, 1973, p. 124; 79: Kate Stephenson, courtesy Yestermorrow Archives; 81–82: DeWalt.

Process
01–02, 04, 08–09, 19–20, 25–28: NDBS Archives; 03, 23: Kathy Meyer; 05, 07: Steve Badanes; 06: Charlie Hailey; 10: Jake LaBarre, courtesy NDBS Archives; 11–13, 15–18, 24: Jim Adamson, Rocco Ceo; 14: Jim Adamson; 21–22: Yestermorrow Archives.

Lessons
01–02: UW CBE Visual Resources Collection; 03–04, 09: NBDS Archives; 05–08, 15–17: Steve Badanes and Jim Adamson; 10, 12: Steve Badanes; 11, 13–14: Yestermorrow Archives.

Cases
Rural Kitchen
All figures courtesy Tiffany Chu, Sam Cohen, Lee Dyxkhoorn, Adam Galletly, Julie Gawendo, Rebecca Gould, Alorah Harman, Lisa Hedstrom, Kleindienst, Ethan Lacy, Zachary Lamb, Andrea Love, Joseph Nunez, Lisa Pauli, Pamela Ritchot, Sian Siobhan Rockcastle, Julianna Sassaman, Yan-Ping Wang.

Urban Farm Supershed
All figures courtesy NDBS Archives.

Home Design/Build Outbuildings
03: Yumiko Virant; 17: Tom Virant; 21: Yestermorrow Archives. All others courtesy David Bosco.

ACKNOWLEDGMENTS

DISCLAIMER

This project grew out of the work of Jersey Devil. I thank Jim, John, and Steve for their vital contributions, mentorship, friendship, and lasting inspiration. From footing to peak, they have helped build this project. Marielle Suba has been instrumental in crafting this book with indispensable creative insight, editorial input, and logistical support; and I thank Megan Carey for significant feedback in the project's early stages. Bahar Aktuna provided essential research support throughout the project's final year. The following have also generously assisted and contributed to the project: Samuel Batchelor, Linda Beaumont, Bill Bialosky, Rocco Ceo, Daniel Claro, Amy Creekmur, Michael Crosbie, Lee Dykxhoorn, Miriam Gee, Aidan Hailey, Phoebe Hailey, Jan Haux, Melanie Hobson, Magdalena Hogness, Howard S. Wright Endowment, Jake LaBarre, Ethan Lacy, Zach Lamb, Kevin Lang, Kathy Meyer, Ashley Muse, Susan Piedmont-Palladino, Dávila Parker-García, Joshua Polansky, Jared Polesky, Amanda Reed, Bill Sanders, Jason Sawyer, Gus Sinsheimer, Kate Stephenson, University of Florida College of DCP and Office of Research, University of Washington College of Built Environments.

Please don't try anything you see in this book unless you're completely certain that you can do it safely.

Published by
Princeton Architectural Press
A McEvoy Group company
37 East Seventh Street
New York, New York 10003

Visit our website at www.papress.com

Editor: Marielle Suba
Designer: Jan Haux

Special thanks to: Nicola Bednarek Brower, Janet Behning,
Erin Cain, Tom Cho, Barbara Darko, Benjamin English,
Jenny Florence, Jan Cigliano Hartman, Lia Hunt, Mia Johnson,
Valerie Kamen, Simone Kaplan-Senchak, Stephanie Leke,
Diane Levinson, Jennifer Lippert, Sara McKay, Jaime Nelson Noven,
Rob Shaeffer, Sara Stemen, Paul Wagner, Joseph Weston, and
Janet Wong of Princeton Architectural Press
—Kevin C. Lippert, publisher

Library of Congress Cataloging-in-Publication Data

Names: Hailey, Charlie, 1970- author.
Title: Design/build with Jersey Devil : a handbook for education and practice
   / Charlie Hailey.
Description: First edition. | New York : Princeton Architectural Press, 2016.
   | Includes bibliographical references.
Identifiers: LCCN 2015046496 | ISBN 9781616893569 (paperback)
Subjects: LCSH: Architecture—Philosophy. | Building—Philosophy. | Jersey
   Devil (Firm) | BISAC: ARCHITECTURE / Design, Drafting, Drawing &
   Presentation. | ARCHITECTURE / Buildings / General. | ARCHITECTURE /
   Adaptive Reuse & Renovation.
Classification: LCC NA2500 .H233 2016 | DDC 720.1—dc23
LC record available at http://lccn.loc.gov/2015046496

Jersey Devil, summer 2015.

To tell the truth, I simply enjoy making things and teaching other people how to make things.
—Leon Barth